Discerning the Signs of the Times and the Church's Reformation

by Samuel Willard
with chapters by C. Matthew McMahon

Copyright Information

Discerning the Signs of the Times and the Church's Reformation
by Samuel Willard, with chapters by C. Matthew McMahon
Edited by Therese B. McMahon

Copyright ©2020 by Puritan Publications and A Puritan's Mind®

Some language and grammar have been updated from original manuscripts. Any change in wording or punctuation has not changed the intent or meaning of the original author(s) and has been made to aid the modern reader with gently updated language.

Published by Puritan Publications
A Ministry of A Puritan's Mind® in Crossville, TN.
www.apuritansmind.com
www.puritanpublications.com

All rights reserved. No part of this publication may be reproduced, stored in a retrieval system or transmitted in any form by any means, electronic, mechanical, photocopy, recording or otherwise, without the prior permission of the publisher, except as provided by USA copyright law.

This Print Edition, 2020
Electronic Edition, 2020

Manufactured in the United States of America

ISBN: 978-1-62663-365-0
eISBN: 978-1-62663-364-3

Table of Contents

Meet Samuel Willard..4
Glamourizing Reform..8

Rules for the Discerning of the Present Times..........18
    Doctrine 1..20

Reformation, the Great Duty of an Afflicted People 45
    Doctrine 1..52
    Doctrine 2..59
    Doctrine 3..66
    Doctrine 4..72
    Doctrine 5..78
    Doctrine 6..84
    Doctrine 7..92
    Doctrine 8..97

Other Helpful Books on Reformation by Puritan Publications...106

Meet Samuel Willard
by C. Matthew McMahon Ph.D., Th.D.

Samuel Willard (1640-1707) was born in Concord, Massachusetts, and has been deemed "the last puritan." However, on two accounts this would be untrue. First, *puritanism* surrounds those nonconformist ministers who remained *in* the Church of England in order to "purify it." Secondly, those ministers who left the Church of England were called *pilgrims*, not puritans. Certainly, Willard's doctrine was in fair *accordance* with Puritanism, and the Reformed Theology of the day (as was Jonathan Edwards later), but historically speaking, it would be better to deem Mr. Willard a reformed Preacher of the Gospel, than "a puritan."

Willard attended Harvard and graduated in 1659, studying divinity after his conversion to the Gospel. After graduating from Harvard, he was ordained a minister in Groton, Massachusetts in 1664,[1] where he served as pastor until 1676 (until the town was attacked by Indians in 1676, during King Philip's War). He was then called to the Old South Church in Boston, and became the second most important preacher of the New England Calvinistic Church of the day, after Increase Mather (1639-1723). John Dunton (1659-1733), an English bookseller, said, "He's a man of profound notions, can say what he will, and prove what he says," commenting on Willard's scholarly abilities with Scripture. He had a keen ability for preaching with excellent delivery. For example, his son-in-law, Rev. Samuel Neal, preached for him in the Old South church one Lord's Day, and the sermon being considered very poor, the congregation requested that he should not be invited to fill the pulpit again. Mr. Willard borrowed the identical sermon and *read* it to the same congregation, but with more skill, which immediately requested a copy for publication.

Willard strenuously opposed the Salem witchcraft trials and tried to influence public opinion against them.

---

[1] In 1664 he married Abigail Sherman of Watertown, Massachusetts.

When Increase Mather retired from the presidency of Harvard, Mr. Willard, being vice-president, succeeded to the government of that college, serving in 1701 until 1707.

In keeping with a Reformed emphasis on the Gospel, Willard's preaching centered on the doctrine of the *covenant*.[2] He opposed Arminianism by preaching the Reformed doctrines of predestination, total depravity, limited atonement, irresistible grace, and perseverance of the saints as standards of Gospel truth, consistently magnifying the sovereignty of God's divine grace through Jesus Christ's redemptive work.

Willard rightly opposed Antinominanism by writing and preaching vigorously on the historic Reformed emphases of revelation, justification, and sanctification. Throughout his ministry he propagated and defended New England's biblical and orthodox stance on infant baptism, an educated pastorate, and the alliance of church and state in religion (rightly opposing both Baptist and Quaker theology).

Willard published many sermons including one of the largest books ever printed in New England, *A Compleat Body of Divinity*.[3]

---

[2] His work "The Doctrine of the Covenant of Redemption," masterfully demonstrates this, which has been republished by Puritan Publications.

[3] This book was influential on the next generation of ministers in New England, including Solomon Stoddard and Stoddard's grandson, Jonathan Edwards. It was the largest printed work in New England at the time, and was published by two of Willard's pastoral colleagues from the old South Church after his death.

Some of his most famous sermons and works include:

1. "A Sermon occasioned by the Death of John Leverett, Governor of Massachusetts" (Boston, 1679).
2. "The Duty of a People that have renewed their Covenant with God," (1680).
3. "Ne Sutor ultra Crepidam, or Brief Animadversions upon the New England Anabaptists' Late Fallacious Narrative," (1681).
4. "Mourner's Cordial against Excessive Sorrow," (1691).
5. "Peril of the Times displayed, or Rules for the discerning of the present times" (1700).
6. "Compleat Body of Divinity," 250 sermons organized according to the *Westminster Shorter Catechism*.
7. "Reformation, the Great Duty of an Afflicted People," (1694).

Glamourizing Reform
by C. Matthew McMahon, Ph.D., Th.D.

History cannot be documented simply as chronological events, but the intrusion of God into time to establish his redemptive purposes by Christ in and through sinful men. Two ages in this Spirit's work to apply the glorious merit of the Christ to fallen men point to the greatest revolutions ever documented. Certainly, the first epoch is the entrance of the Lord of glory in the fullness of time in the little town of Bethlehem. In this, the Christ came to save his people from their sins. He is *the Savior*, sent by the Father from before the foundation of the world to bring salvation to a wayward people, and by his coming in the fullness of time, he instituted the greatest reformation of men's souls ever seen. His power was and is fall-reversing in this way and changes man's very heart from a heart of stone to a heart of flesh. He reforms men by his Spirit, from being dead in sin to being alive in him, "as those that are alive from the dead, and your members as instruments of righteousness unto God," (Rom. 6:13).

The second era in which we find Reformation, is when the Gospel broke out of a reign of eclipsing doctrinal darkness and superstition, in the magisterial Reformation. Christ brought forth the good tidings of God, and the Reformers rescued this Gospel from drowning in a sea of ecclesiastical expedience. Since the Gospel writers, carried along by the Spirit inspired as they were, have given an accurate account of the life of Christ and the early church, in today's modern age, we ought always to desire to remember the Christ, and remember his providences through rescuing his Gospel that leads to eternal life in the historical work of the Reformation. Christ's reformation gave way to Luther's reformation. Christ's reformation was the foundation and work of Luther's reform. But what kind of reform is this? *Hold that thought for a moment.*

God is not intruding into time merely to arrange events, but to begin *revolutions* that cover over the face of the earth for his glory. Revolution is what the magisterial Reformation was all about. Can you, reader, say the same about your church today? Is your church *revolutionary?* There are churches all over the United States, for example, that have as their name, "Revolution Church." In fact, there is one in my own town with that name. But there is no revival here, or in those towns across the US that we know of. There hadn't been for decades. Would the bygone reformers think of your church as one partaking in *their* revolution, or would your pastor and the people that attend to hear him, say that they exist to meet the needs of the emerging culture that the church today exists in, to be progressive and ever-changing as a church? In contrast to the Reformation, the emergent church movement today is a heretical band of incompetents, and in its teachings they have given up completely on the Gospel, and instead, they have emerged in the culture with a socialized kind of "happy news" that will meet people where they are both socially and financially in their cultural distress. People just want to be loved for who they are no matter what they do. And this emerging church is a kind of reform today that is a glamourizing of the word "reform" but has nothing to do with its biblical connotation.

Though God has his providential hand in the affairs of Alexander the Great, or World War 2, as well as in the life of the apostle Paul, the greater question that should concern the Christian surrounds the *remedy of the fallen soul* by Jesus Christ, the one and only Mediator of God, as he works within the ever-moving dimension of time. To truly document history is to set one's historical eye on the Gospel of Christ and its affects on the world as it converts sinners into saints. The Reformation, at its time, would bring back justification by faith alone, where the popes have set up a capitalistic endeavor to make faith something to be bought, and achieved by works, set under the thumb of the Antichrist. The *indulgence* of their day rapidly affected those who were superstitious that had already been familiar to a submission of their will under the one claiming to be the Vicar of Christ on earth (absurdity at its highest!). The clergy had become the conduits by which the grace of God, or really the favor of the popes, was to be dispensed. The works of bygone saints, even the supererogatory merits of Jesus Christ, could be *bought* for a price in order to secure the salvation of the buyer, or aid in the release of those already captive to the purging of sin in purgatory. Financial advantage to the Roman Church did not go unnoticed, and purgatory became one of the chief doctrines to validate indulgences in the thirteenth century, and to furnish the livelihood of the papal Antichrist.

The Reformation brought man face to face with God rather than having popery "interpose the Church between God and man." Popery separates men from God and hides the Gospel from them, where the Reformation, through the true Gospel of Jesus Christ, and justification by faith alone, will unite men to God in godly reform. Does your church bring men face to face with the Jesus Christ of the Bible and of the Reformation, or does your pastor meet the needs of the people in his sermons? Does your church hold steadfastly to the doctrines taught by Christ, and later by the Reformation, or just those that your church and pastor deem convenient? And what about you, reader? Are you a *closet* reformist? Or are you a *true revolutionary?*

I can hear you now. You've seen the *Luther* movie. Yes, you are very sure you would shake your fist and stand your ground amidst such opposition if "you were in his shoes at the time." You'd say the same things and borrow the same lines Luther did … right? Would the people in your church, at your work, in your family, amidst your friends say the same things *about* you? Would they say *you are a revolutionary* in the same light as the reformation? Has Jesus Christ radically transformed you to really act in accordance with godliness, perpetually and universally in your character and conduct? I know, you would admit, you are no Luther or Calvin. That's not *your* place, right? That's for your *pastor* to emulate. You are just a simple hardworking Christian. You are just trying to get through the day at work, and get through a simple devotion time with your family. You don't have the time to be a *revolutionary*.

    The Reformation had made its way from the minds of a few men zealous for the truth, to the practical application of the doctrines they represented in the life of the church. People lived out, at that time, upon pain of death, their Christianity. Yes, in some places in countries that are communist, they still do that today. But there is no fist shaking there, and no councils. They just murder them for being a Christian. They shoot them, behead them, and run over them with steam rollers (and they really do that). I know, I know, *your persecution* doesn't extend that far. We aren't speaking about when you "get a flat tire" and "feel God is against you today," or when your "pool pump breaks" *again*. We are talking about, however, the reality behind a true Christianity and the fall-reversing power of reformation. "The Reformation," you might think? No, actually, not necessarily "The Magisterial Reformation," just plain, everyday *reformation of life*. That's where revolutionaries live every moment. You may not have to worry so much about being persecuted for your faith in the US (and I can only speak about where I live), because, as you already admitted to yourself, you are not really a revolutionary "like that." You loved to watch the *Luther Movie* each year because it causes you to get emotionally high on the thoughts and glamor of the initial *sparks* of the Reformation. But far be it for you to challenge your church on whether or not it really falls in line with the Reformation, and with the Gospel they preached. Far be it that you incite a *reformation of life* in your church. Was that what the reformers were doing in their day? Was it really that the "Reformation" wanted to see "sanctification" in the life of the church, day to day? What movie did *Luther* watch to get emotionally excited about reform? Or, was it that he was just studying his bible? What was behind the second reformation of the puritans when they bound together under a solemn league and covenant, a holy vow, to set down what manner all the church in England, Ireland and Scotland would follow for worship ... for church government ... for family worship ... for personal prayer?

Remember when I said to *hold that thought?* Let's continue that thought. Christ's revolution came in order to usher in the fulness of the Kingdom. It changes sinners to live for him who is the Great King. His revolution is continued in them day to day. So, here is the difference between your "reformation ideas" and "The Magisterial Protestant Reformation," or even the further reformation of such as the Puritans at the assembly of divines at Westminster: you enjoy the emotional high that you get when you think about when other Christians in bygone eras did something you believe was great, and you wished you could do that too; but ... *at a distance.* You certainly might have ideas that coincide with those reformers which you may hold dear about Jesus. But if your personal reformation is as revolutionary or radical as theirs was, would you lose your job for your beliefs? Would your pastor be willing to be thrown out of his church for teaching the Regulative Principle in distinction to all the other churches in his circles that "take exceptions" to holy worship? Would it be okay if your family was divided as a result of the truths you hold so dear, as long as Christ was being glorified in the truth? If you really embrace the reformation as a *revolutionary*, how can things like that *not* happen? And I speak as one who has indeed been thrown, literally, out of a church for teaching that men are sinners at conception and under the curse of the fall. I don't say that to boast, but simply to show you that things like that happen today to those who profess to hold to the good tidings of the Great King.

True biblical reformation is not the same as *merely remembering* what Luther or Calvin did. Reformation occurs when the discerning Christian *takes to heart* what Christ has commanded them to do as their duty in obedience to him as their great King *day in and day out.* We often glamourize the Reformation because we don't connect the reality that reformation is to be done every single day of the year until we die, until we are brought to heaven. It is a daily occurrence, and it is not as easy as we think. In *truly remembering* the Reformation historically, one has no choice but to practically apply it as a revolutionary today in their daily walk. Is the Reformation just a picture in a book, or a scene from a movie? Or is it *real* to you, embraced by you, propagated through you and lived out because the bible is *all about personal reform?* Jesus Christ didn't come to earth to die for sinners so that they can disparage his commands, or become lazy in their walk. He requires their *allegiance* once they are born again to the *perpetual and universal obedience to his word in both character and conduct.* "Thou shalt love the Lord thy God with *all* thy heart, and with *all* thy soul, and with *all* thy mind. This is the first and great commandment," (Matt. 22:37-38).

It may be that you bought this little work by Willard because it had "something to do" with "Reformation" and you *like books about reformation.* It does refer to that. But Willard is going to place the idea of reformation into the discerning hands of the Christian, who desires reformation *in the biblical sense.* His main doctrine (though he has 8) is that *the great design of all God's judgments on a professing people is to reform them.* That sounds a bit negative. Judgment? It is the plight of the church that they live in light of the fall of Adam. They strive for holiness, but they must be very discerning about the times in which they live, so that they may set themselves steadfastly in the work of personal reform, church reform, and world reform to the glory of God. This is not something to just think about in October as some supposed *Reformation Month*. It is something they do every minute of every day until God decides it is time for death to take them and bring them to heaven. And if they do not do it, if they neglect Christ's commands, if they willfully sin against God day in and day out, God brings them a forced reform, or a certain judgment on them.

So, this work is not about glamorizing the Protestant Reformation. It is about holding to biblical reformation, and seeing fruit in reform day by day. Willard explains Matthew 16:3, "Ye hypocrites, Ye can discern the face of the sky, but can ye not discern the signs of the times?" He does this in order to press the Christian to be discerning in the day in which he lives. What is God doing? Where is God working? What are the signs of the times saying *to the church?* And then he explains Leviticus 26:23, "If ye will not be reformed by me by these things, but will walk contrary unto me, then will I also walk contrary unto you, and will punish you yet seven times for your sins." First, the Christian is discerning the times, and then the Christian is reforming in those times. All of God's providences stretch forth from his covenant blessing to bring his wayward people back to a right relationship with him. He reforms them so that they become real revolutionaries for his cause; and his cause is holiness of life. A modern church that remains unreformed with a professing people who walk contrary to God's word, there Christ will proceed in his judgments against them and strike them with blows to bring them back to him and true faith. What calamities have been brought on the church today in this? It seems Willard is striking at the heart of the church currently during the pandemic, calamities, famines, riots, and a number of other difficulties that our country, and many countries around the world, are currently experiencing. But make a course correction in this. These things have been brought in by the church. And the content of this work is so current, one would have thought Willard preached these discourses just last Lord's Day.

May you be helped by Willard in this work as you strive for true reformation, day to day, to the glory of Christ, and not merely the glamourizing of history that is far out of the reach of most professors of religion.

In the grace of the Lord Jesus Christ,
C. Matthew McMahon, Ph.D. Th.D.,
From my study, July, 2020.

Rules for the Discerning of the Present Times[4]

"Ye hypocrites, Ye can discern the face of the sky, but can ye not discern the signs of the times?" (Matthew 16:3).

The occasion of these words, spoken by Christ himself to the Pharisees and Sadducees, we shall find in history. We read at the latter end of the foregoing chapter, that Christ had been showing his divine power in a miraculous feeding of a multitude with a few loaves and fishes. One would have thought he had sufficiently convinced them who he was, even the expected Messiah. On this, in the beginning of this chapter, we have the Pharisees and Sadducees coming to him, and asking a sign of him, (verse 1). And this was just at the time as he had been giving of them an eminent sign. Unbelief makes men so impertinent. Our Savior, on this, very suitably, in verses 2-3 sharply reproves them for not making use of those signs which they had. And this reproof he establishes on the consideration of their curiosity in observing, and aptness to conclude from their observation of natural and fallible signs with respect to fair and foul weather. This he sets in conjunction with their dullness and incogitance in observing, and incredulity in concluding about greater,

---

[4] *Rules for the Discerning of the Present Times Recommended to the People of God, in New-England.* Preached on the Lecture in Boston; November 27th, 1692 by Samuel Willard. Eccl. 8:5, "A Wise man's heart discerneth both time and judgment." (Boston, MA: Printed by Benjamin Harris, 1693).

and more momentous affairs, in other words, the signs of the times.

Our text is the explanation of this comparison, or the conviction itself which he applies from the foregoing consideration.

In the words then we may observe these two things.

1. An offensive title which he puts on them, "O ye hypocrites." A hypocrite is one that makes a fair and dissembling show of something that he does not intend. These men pretended to have an earnest desire of being informed about Christ and his authority, but it was a mere presence they sought.

2. The ground or reason of this offensive title, "Ye can discern," *etc.* The sum is, that they had studied and obtained skill in a matter of so little importance, and yet were unacquainted with things of the highest concernment, *viz.*, the signs of the times.

A *sign* is something that represents some other thing to us, and gives us some notification about it. We are by it instructed about something else and we may from it receive information, make observation, and draw conclusions accordingly.

Now these signs are either natural, or positive and instituted. Natural signs are such as have in them a natural connection with the thing signified, or the reason of the signification is in their nature. Such were these in the sky here mentioned. In this way, natural causes are signs of those effects that are indicated by them. So, proper accidents are signs of their subjects; and many are like these. Positive or instituted signs are such as are so made by appointment, which puts their signification into them; and they can be either of God or of man. If they are of man's appointment, this was like Rahab's *scarlet thread* to be a sign to the spies, (Joshua 2:18). If they are of God's appointment, they are like the rainbow which was given to Noah, (Gen. 9:12-13), and circumcision to Abraham (Genesis 17:10) as a sign. In this way, all those things which the Scripture predicted should come to pass, either as forerunners, or concomitants of Christ's coming and appearance in the flesh, were to be signs by which men were to know it, and to judge of it. And these seem to be more peculiarly the things which Christ aims at in our text.

There are also mixed and moral signs, which are partly of institution, and partly have a moral influence into the things which they signify; and have a real signification in them.

By the *signs of the times* we may here understand such tokens by which we are advantaged to judge what times we are fallen into, and what prognostics may be made of them, on a moral account.

The word here used for *discerning*, is of a middle signification; it is sometimes used for debating and hesitating in a matter that is dubious and we are at a loss to determine about it; and sometimes for judging rationally of things, and drawing conclusions from premises, whether probable or certain, according to the force there appears to be in them. It is in this latter sense, we are here to take it. *Therefore,*

DOCTRINE 1:

It is an important duty lying on the people of God to labor after a skill in discerning the signs of the times which they live in.

Our Savior here upbraids these Pharisees, who were men that pretended to be high in religion, and would be thought to out-do others in their knowledge and practice, yet they were unacquainted in this great affair. They were times in which men were in great expectation, and yet they did not understand these signal discoveries which God then made in his providence.

The importance of this *duty* will briefly appear, if we lay these things together.

1. That there are varieties of times which pass over men. The times are not always alike, there are good days, and there are evil days. There is a day of prosperity, and a day of adversity. There is a time of peace and a time of trouble. The wise man makes such an observation as this in Ecclesiastes, and they are the various aspects of God's providence on men that make these differences in the times. For, it is he who orders all the changes that go over men, whether public or private. This truth David confesses in, Psa. 31:15, "My times are in thy hand."

2. That there are signs of these times. God is accustomed frequently to fore-signify to men what revolutions there are likely to come on them. There are certain indications or forerunning symptoms, which as they intimate what the present times are, and what remarks are to be made upon them, so they carry in them the prognostic of what days are coming. As to natural

signs which some pretend to from astrological observations, and predictions grounded on these, I do not meddle with them, nor is there any credit to be given to those that do; and it is to be lamented that so many Christians are seduced into a good opinion of them. But, as to moral and instituted signs, they are such as God himself has therefore appointed in his word because he would have men to improve them. Therefore, it is his command, Jer. 10:2, "Learn not the way of the heathen, and be not dismayed at the signs of heaven." So, also, we have the complaint of the church in Psalm 74:9, "We see not our signs." These signs are capable of being discerned, not only the things themselves that are signs may be known, but under this consideration as they are so, *i.e.* there may be a discovery made of the thing signified by them. The very reason why God has appointed them to be signs, is that men may so be instructed by them; and on this they would lose their end of being so, if they were not to be understood. Nor, yet would men come under blame from God for their lack in discerning them, as they do. There are, therefore, such rules given us in the word of God as are for our discretion in this regard, and according to which we may and ought to judge of the times; only if we would not mistake or fall short in our judgment, and be led into error. We must be critical, and take pains in the application of these rules.

4. There are special duties relating to these times as they are circumstanced. As the disposing of the times according to his holy pleasure, is one part of the government of the world by God; so, as they have any

reference to mankind, they have a respect to his special government, which always has an eye to the law of that government, according unto which God manages the affairs of this sort of beings, and for that reason there is a moral consideration to be had of them. This is because they have a regard to the rule of relative justice, which God has fixed. For this it follows, that there are moral duties to be particularly inferred from them. There is a voice in every turn of providence which passes over men, and it speaks to them, signifying what it is that God requires of them at such a time, and it highly concerns them to hear it, so that they may practice accordingly. And these duties vary as to their specialty, as the times vary, so consider Eccl. 7:14, "In the day of prosperity rejoice; and in the days of adversity consider."

5. The way for men to know these duties is *by* discerning the times. It is true, there are the general duties of religion which are accommodated to all times, we are to trust in God at all times, and whatever difficulties and darknesses are on us, we are to pray evermore. We are not to be discouraged at anything that would persuade us that God does not hear us. We are, without ceasing, to serve the lord with fear, and rejoice with trembling. These duties can never be out of season, no matter what the times are. But there are more particular engagements lying on us, which are urged from the times, and there are more arguments to press them on us gathered from those times. There is a present work to be done, something that God now more eminently calls for, and it is pointed to by the time itself. Here is that reproof given to them in Jer. 8:7, "Yea the

stork in the heavens knoweth her appointed times," *etc.* "but my people know not the judgments of the Lord." Now, if men do not regard, and on this are unacquainted with the time, how shall they understand what this duty is that they are now to set upon?

6. The consequence of doing or neglecting these duties is very great. A people's happiness or misery depends on it. A mistake here may prove woefully hazardous to men. If the times for the present are good, they may be either continued or lost, accordingly as men improve them. We may observe what a threatening God utters against them, Deut. 28:47-48, "Because thou servedst not the Lord with joyfulness and gladness of heart, for the abundance of all things, therefore shalt thou serve thine enemies." If the times are bad, and men do not carry an answer to them, but walk contrarily, it is the way to make them worse. Hear what God says, Isa. 22:12-13, "In that day the Lord of hosts called to weeping," *etc.* "And behold joy and gladness," *etc.* Surely this iniquity shall not be purged from you until you die. No, if bad times are fore-boded and predicted, men may either precipitate or avert them by their answerable demeanor. How eminently is this exemplified in the men of Nineveh, (Jonah 3). And the truth is, men may thank themselves, if after their being in this way forewarned, they yet fall into mischief, they might have prevented it, if they had attended the voice of providence, and known the day of their visitation. Hear that expostulation, Isaiah 48:18-19, "Oh that thou hadst hearkened to my commandments, then had thy peace been as a river," *etc.* They prove themselves to be but simple fools; for what

does the wise man say in Prov. 27:12? "The prudent foreseeth the evil and hideth himself, but the simple passeth on and is punished." So, then, the case I am here to endeavor to give some resolution of is the following.

Question. By what rules may we truly and profitably discern the present times?

Answer. Here let me premise the following.

1. That this case may be applied to the prophetical times mentioned in the scriptures, which respect that glorious state of the church which is believed and expected by the servants of God, in the latter days. That there shall be such a time; that it is stated and determined in the counsel of God; that there are the signs of its approaching; that the day of it is coming on apace; and that it is our duty soberly to acquaint ourselves with the tokens of it, the word of God is our warrant, nor ought they who fear God in New England to look on themselves or theirs as unconcerned in it, because they dwell in a remote corner of the earth. But I shall altogether wave this in the present enquiry.

2. It might also be extended generally to the whole affair of the people of God in the world at this day, and it would be a profitable speculation; for if we are bound to pray for the peace of Jerusalem, we ought then to be very inquisitive after the condition which the church is in. This is so we may accordingly direct our petitions to God in its behalf and understand what answer our prayers do receive from him, and to neglect it will argue that we are but a little concerned about them. But I shall not directly intend this either; although the rules to be given may be generally applicable. *So:*

3. I shall direct the resolution of this case more especially to ourselves, or this little company of a professing people, in this nook or corner of the world; and let it here be observed, that although, not only Christ's mystical body is but one, but also the visible church of Christ on earth is in some respects but one too, since they do or ought to profess the same God, the same Christ, the same faith, the same ordinances, and consequently are subjects of the same government of Christ. Yet, as they are dispersed up and down in diverse places of the world; and on this are severally combined, the times may be exceedingly diversified to them, and consequently the signs are very various. Religion may flourish in this place, and it may at the same time be under great decays in another; here there may be good, and there may be bad symptoms. Nor does this only respect particular churches, or congregations, although these also may be very unlike them, but the collective body of them too, as they are involved in a more immediate communion one with another in sacred and civil respects. For God is accustomed to treat with them in his providence under the consideration of such a people so combined, as is evidently to be observed from the word of God.

Signs, according to the scriptural use of the word, are by critics ranked under three heads. 1. Indicative or notifying signs. Such as carry in them a discovery of the present state of affairs, and tell men what they are to judge of things as they now are; or give light for a prediction of some future events, having a reason in them for this conclusion, whether natural or moral from which men may raise a conjecture of what is near at hand, or in great likelihood shortly to come to pass. Such are the signs *of the sky* taken notice of in the text. In this way the death of Hophni and Phinehas in one day, were a sign to Eli of the accomplishment of all that God had threatened against his family, (1 Sam. 2:34). "This shall be a sign unto thee." 2. Monitory; *viz.,* such as carry moral instruction in them to others, and bid them to beware. In this way the judgments of God which befall some sinners for notorious sins, are signs to others, admonishing them to consider what they came for, and beware of exposing themselves to the like judgments by like sins, lest they also suffer as those did. In this way Korah and his accomplices are said to be made a sign in Israel, (Num. 26:10), and thus God threatens them to make them a sign and a proverb, (Ezek. 14:8). 3. For the confirmation of things done. There are ratifying signs. In this way a man's setting of his hand to a deed is called his *signing of it*, and so circumcision is called a sign, it being given for a ratification of the covenant which God made with Abraham, (Rom. 4:11). But this last one is not so much of our present consideration; it being the former which the case in hand has a more peculiar relation to it.

    Now that we may have a right discerning of the present times, there are two things which call for our observation. 1. What times are new on us? 2. What aspects there is on those times? Or what are the symptoms, and what are prognostics of the present times?

Rules for Discerning of the Present Times

1. What times are now on us? And this may come under either a physical or moral consideration. And both of them call for our observation.

1. In a physical consideration, times are to be accounted either as good or bad, according to the dispensations of providence in mercies or afflictions. There is indeed for the most part a mixture of these, it is seldom that times are so good, as that it can be said of a people, as it was once of them, (1 Kings 5:4). There is neither adversary, nor evil occurrent. Nor is it ordinary, but that the greatest affliction are tempered with a mixture of many mercies, so that a judgment is here to be made according to the prevalent degree of either and by this rule, it is now certainly an evil day with this people. It is beyond question a time of trouble; and I think I have no need to go about to reason them into a belief of this assertion, of which there are so many sensible demonstrations. And without a doubt *sense* is a competent judge of sensible evils. Surely seeing and feeling is believing in such a case. There is no persuading of one who is under the apprehension of acute pains which make him to roar, that all is well with him. I may then pass over this as a thing beyond doubt.

2. In a moral consideration, and here the great enquiry will be, whether these afflictions under which we are, are merely probationary, or not also penal? There is a very great difference between these two, and there are signs by which it is to be proved, and according to which a judgment is to be made. A mistake here is dangerous, since there are duties incumbent on us,

referring to our state in these respects. To help us in this regard let us observe the following.

    1. I suppose that the rule which many take up with, *viz.*, that private or personal afflictions may be for a trial, but that public calamities are always punishments, or chastisement for sin, will not hold universally. It may possibly be true for the most part, but it may not be fixed for a *certain unerring rule*. That God has tied himself up to this way of proceeding is hard to determine, since there may be a reason given for his so dealing in way of trial with a people, as well as with a person. Nor am I able to give any other account of that remarkable passage referring to Hezekiah, (2 Chron. 32:1, "After these things and the establishment of them, Senacherib king of Assyria came and entered into Judah, and encamped against the fenced cities," *etc.* When was this, but after Hezekiah had worked an eminent reformation, and settled the matters of religion in the kingdom? And that in Asa's reign recorded, (2 Chron. 16:1ff) seems to carry the same face on it; just before, in chapter 15:17, God had testified that the heart of Asa was "perfect all his days." Without a doubt there are follies in the best times, but God does not impute them, or chide for them, or take the advantage of them to enter into controversies with his people, (Psalm 130:3-4).

    2. Public calamities may sometimes be the punishments of some sins that have been long before committed. God is pleased in his sovereignty sometimes to reserve his testimony against them until afterwards, yes, until they that were the principals in committing them are dead and gone. So, a people may be called to

look a great way back, if they would find out what is the sign in this respect.

There was a famine which came upon Israel in David's reign, (2 Sam 24:1ff). But on inquiry, it was found to be for act of unjust cruelty which Saul had committed in his reign. God tells Moses that he will remember the sin of making the golden calf *afterwards*, (Exod. 32:34). Where the Jews have a proverb, that in every judgment that after befell them, there was an ounce of the calf. And it is very important, that if there had been no public testimony of repentance for such sins as the public has been involved in, they have just ground to believe that God is in such afflictions calling of those sins to remembrance, and visiting for them.

3. Afflictions that are penal, usually come on a generation, for the sins of the generation that is so afflicted. It is true, and it often so comes to pass, that their sins may be *filling sins.* What does Christ say to the Jews of his time? (Matt. 23:32), "fill up the measure of your fathers." But however, God himself has given us to understand, that if the children observe their father's sins, and take warning by them, and repent thoroughly, this shall be prevented, (Ezek. 18:14), *etc.* So that the reason is because they pursue the same refractory courses, until the "ephah is full." And so, these are the sins that pull down the anger of God. Now there are these three signs by which we may discern that the calamities on a people are not mere trials, but the effects of divine displeasure, and say, that God who sends them is angry with such a people.

1). If they are guilty of apparent and sensible apostasy. If a people that walk close with God, and maintain the life of religion in their profession, are notwithstanding in this way oppressed with troubles, they may take this for a trial, and accordingly improve it. But if there are notorious decays and too general declinings either in the duties themselves, or in the zealous pursuit and practice of them, an increase of sin among them, and now calamities come on them, it shows that God is angry, and that he is now punishing them for these things; for this is according to the threatenings which he has pronounced. If Ephesus departs from her first love, and neglects her first works, she by this endangers the removing of the candlestick, (Rev. 2:3-4).

2). If God has stirred up his servants to bear witness against these acts of apostasy, and they are not by them reformed, God is accustomed to warn a professing people before he strikes them; and if his warnings are suitably entertained, they are to end there, and the compliance of such a people with them, are used to avert the evil against them. Yes, though he has proceeded to severe threatenings against them, yet, in this way, there may be a stop put to their execution, (Jer. 18:7-8). It is God's way to send messages by his servants, whom he has made sensible of the decays under which a people are fallen, and to stir up a holy zeal in them to bear witness against such back-slidings; if these are despised, or not regarded, and the people are not convinced and awakened and reformed, but they hold on in their evil courses, and it may be decline yet more after all, and there is no appearance of any likelihood that it should be otherwise. And now calamities come on them and this can be judged to be no other but the confirmation of his word in the mouth of his messengers. This, therefore, is given as a reason of their miseries, Jer. 44:4-6, "Howbeit I sent unto you all my servants the prophets, rising early and sending them, saying, Oh do not this abominable thing that I hate. But they hearkened not," *etc.* "Wherefore my fury and mine anger was poured forth," *etc.*

3). If they were not reclaimed by the higher and easier afflictions which they felt. God, for the most part, uses them to proceed gradually, and when he has laid some more gentle strokes on a sinning people that would not be warned to prevent them. He hearkens to hear if they will not lay these to heart, and receive instruction by it, so as to be reformed, Jer. 8:6, "I hearkened and heard." But if they do not regard these, they do not take their hint, but still turn to their old course, and there follow more grievous and distressing troubles, these are judgments and the manifest fruits of his anger. And this also is consonant to the rule which God has given us of his proceeding in this case, Lev. 26:18, "And if ye will not for all this hearken unto me, then I will punish you seven times more for your sins."

By these rules a people may know themselves to be under the impressions of divine anger, and that God is undoubtedly managing a controversy with them. And they are *sure* signs.

2. What aspect is there on these times? There are signs by which we are to judge, not only what the times are at present, but also what is their tendency, or what prospect we may have for the future of the state of our affairs. And this is an enquiry which everyone is apt enough to be solicitous and anxious about, that is under the apprehension of the present distress. Who is not ready to ask, what hopes there are that the storm will blow over; or must we expect the continuance and increase of our troubles? And to those that make this enquiry for good ends, and with a heart desirous to comply with God in his pleasure, I shall take leave to offer some general rules which may be improved to satisfaction in this respect.

1. That all the afflictions which befall a people at any time, are brought upon them by God. He challenges himself to be the author of this sort of evil, whenever it befalls anyone. Amos 3:6, "Is there any evil in the city, and the Lord hath not done it?" Isa. 45:7, "I form the light, and create darkness; I make peace, and create evil: I the Lord do all these things." There is therefore his wisdom, holiness, righteousness, concerned in it; these are acts of his special government accommodated to its laws. He does these things as he is the judge of the whole earth, and cannot but do right.

2. That all second causes that are used in them, are his instruments, and altogether at his disposal. In these things God uses a mediate providence in which he improves creatures to afflict a sinful people by; and although some of these are causes by counsel, have wills of their own, act on deliberation in their own minds,

have a meaning, and proceed on reasons vastly different from, and contrary to God's design in it. Yet, they are entirely under the management of his providence, as rods and swords; and they can do no more than fulfil his counsel, nor can they go one step farther; such was the Assyrian, Isa. 10:5, 7, "Oh Assyrian the rod of mine anger, and the staff in their hand is mine indignation." However, he does not mean this to be so. So that the whole of these afflictions, and every circumstance in them is ordered and governed by God, not by the will of a man.

3. Here there is nothing signal in them, but what he can alter at pleasure. There is a rational conjecture which men may raise by observing the posture of second causes, from where we may judge of the probabilities of things, and it is in these that carnal wisdom is accustomed to terminate. But, Christians have farther to look; let the aspect of second causes be never so promising, or never so ill boding, from where we are apt either to flatter or frighten ourselves, yet God can turn it about in a moment whenever he is ready. For he has many secret unknown ways he does it in, which cannot possibly be frustrated if once he is resolved. He can make men to change their most obstinate resolutions, as he did by Pharaoh, who had made his heart so hardened against letting Israel go out of his land. He can find men other work to do, which shall divert them, in the very birth of their malicious designs against his people, as he did by Saul, to whom, when he was just ready to seize David, a messenger comes in haste to tell him, the Philistines had invaded the land. He can frighten men

with noises in the air, fill them with panic fears, and put them to run away, as he did by Benhadad's army that beleaguered Samaria, and would else in a very little time have possessed themselves of it, and there are many such things as these with him. These signs therefore, though they are not to be despised, because they are providentially threatening of calamity, yet they ought not to terrify us, because there is a way for them to be remedied. It is by engaging God to take our part; and a people may lay everything on this, Rom. 8:31, "If God be for us, who shall be against us?"

    4. Though God is angry with a sinning people yet he is placable. His anger may be turned away, and his wrath be appeased towards them; though the case be dangerous yet it is not desperate. He is a God of mercy, and there is forgiveness with him that he may be feared. He is a God of compassion, and is prone to pardon, he has relenting bowels, and has exemplified this in remarkable instances, to encourage men to hope in him, notwithstanding their sins have procured his displeasure against them. Even an ungodly Ahab, one who had sold himself to do wickedness, if on the severe threatenings of God declared by the prophet he humbles himself, puts on sackcloth, and walks softly, shall be so far taken notice of, that the judgment shall be deferred as to its complete execution, (1 Kings 21:29). Even an idolatrous and flagitious Nineveh, who were arrived at the height of wickedness, if on the preaching of Jonah, they fast and reform from their debaucheries and oppressions, shall experience his favor. God will repent of the evil which he was ready to bring upon them,

(Jonah 3:9). And what do these stand on record for, but to encourage sinful men, and people to seek God's mercy in the way of a true and thorough repentance?

5. Here he offers fair terms, and makes gracious promises in the case if they are complied with. God is not only accustomed to give men warning of what he is about to do, before he smites them with afflictions, so that they may be cautioned to avoid them, by taking due and proper courses to that end, but he also promises to send them messages when they are under the rod, and feel its pain, in which he invites them to a compliance, with him upon easy and fair terms; assuring them that if they do accept of them he will put a stop to his anger, and return again to them in mercy. And this not once nor twice, but very often. How many such errands, as these were the prophets of old sent on to the people of Israel in evil times? Yes, and when he had so sent them, God hearkened diligently to hear what entertainment they found as one, that would have taken great delight in their good success, (Jer. 8:6).

6. It is of God to work these terms in men, and if sinful people do not comply with them, it is their own fault, and will be charged on them as the fruit of their obstinacy, and rebellious frame of heart. But that they do entertain them is of God's grace. There is in the depraved nature of man a corrupt principle of enmity which sets him against any subjection to the will of God, so that if he leaves men to their own carelessness and stupidity they never will hearken to him; and this dereliction is judicial. But if they are made sensible of their folly, and become willing and obedient, this is the work of his own

Spirit in them. It is the complaint which Moses makes over them, (Deut. 29:3-4), "The great temptations which thine eyes have seen, the signs and the miracles; yet the Lord hath not given you an heart to perceive, and eyes to see, and ears to hear, unto this day; when therefore God invites sinful men to turn to him," it concerns them to pray to him to turn them. So they pray, Psa. 80:1ff, "Turn us again Oh God of our salvation." True repentance, on which these offers of mercy are made to men, is a gift of God; and until he works it in them, all means will fail of effecting it.

7. Here, if God brings them to this, it is a sure sign for good; it is an evidence that will never fail those in whom it is truly to be found. Other grounds of hope, which men are ready to nourish their expectations withal, no, and *very often* do prove to be vain presumptions; but this never will. God for that reason gives a people a heart to turn to him from their backslidings, because he has a mind to return to them in mercy. The promise is full which is in the word of God made to this condition and God would have an afflicted people to try him, and see whether he will fail of his word or not. Mal. 3:10, "Prove me now herewith saith the Lord." Let a people be never so much degenerated, and for it never so sorely distrust, yes, let them be all the black tokens imaginable in the face of providence, of more troubles like to fall on them. Let all the whole course of second causes bode never so ill, yet in all this, let the people humble themselves deeply before him, stir up themselves in good earnest to seek God. If all the orders of men among them do in their places according

to their advantages, set themselves heartily and strenuously to put away the evil that is among them, and amend all their evil ways and doings that have not been good, there is no doubt to be made of it, but that God will save them and do them good. His word is true for it, and he will never recede from it.

8. And until God does this for them, they abide under the threatening. The dealings of God with an heathen world, are upon his mere prerogative, for as they stand in relation to the old covenant, so they are condemned to all misery. Their very lives are spared upon mere indulgence, and he measures out his mercy or his wrath to them in this world according as he sees fit. Where, he treats with a professing people, who are in visible covenant with him, according to the tenor of that covenant, in which there are conditionate promises and threatenings. Now what concerns such a people as they are a body, or a company of professors standing under the obligations of such a covenant, refers to this life and its affairs, for they will not be considered or treated after this life as a people. The terms run in this way here, as we have an account of them, Isa. 1:19-20, "If ye be waking and obedient, ye shall eat the good of the land, but if ye refuse and rebel, ye shall be devoured with the sword," *etc.* Other scriptural expressions exist to the same purpose. As long then as such a people are not worked up to a compliance with these terms on which salvation is promised, the threatening under which they were must continue on them. Therefore, God may do something for them in his sovereignty, which is a liberty which he reserves to himself and sometimes makes use

of it, first to save them, and then to reform them, and make these his mercies to be melting means to bring them to repentance. Ezek. 36:31, "then shall you remember your evil ways," *etc.* (*i.e.* when he had returned and settled them in peace and prosperity). Yet, as to their present state they are a threatened people, and have all reason to expect the judgments of God.

9. Here there are these signs by which we may discern the evil of evil times to be in a likely way to continue and increase.

1. If iniquity abides and abounds among a people after all that God has done. Not that any times are here to be expected so good, as that there shall be no iniquity in them; there will be found some of the worst of men in the best of times and places; but if the same sins which procured the judgments for them, do remain under the same circumstances, or are rather growing into more power and prevalence, (and indeed apostasy is seldom at a stop, until such time as God turns the heart of such a people to himself again, but goes in a gradual progress). We find in this that there is more wrath against them. It is a truth in morals as well as in naturals, that if the cause abides, the effect is not likely to cease. The afflictions which such a people have, are divine testimonies against such sins as God has warned them of, and threatened them for, and they call men to repent of them. And if they do not comply with this call, the provocation continues, and God has said it, that he will go on to punish them, (Lev. 26). If such men should say, is there no peace to be expected, his answer to them would be like his to him in 2 Kings 9:22, "What peace so long as these whoredoms"

abide? And therefore, God pronounces that *woe* upon Jerusalem in Jer. 13:27, "Woe to thee Jerusalem, wilt thou not be made clean? When shall it once be?"

    2. If the affliction that God brings on them makes them worse, instead of reforming them. Those troubles which God brings a professing people into, after such time as warnings and threatenings have been despised by them, do belong to the discipline which he uses with such as are in covenant with him. They are therefore called his corrections, and chastenings. The use, therefore, and improvement which they ought to make of them is to receive instruction by them. They are the tokens and witnesses of God's holy anger, and call on men to see his hand, and seek his reconciliation. And in this way only can they improve them either to God's acceptance, or their own advantage. If then instead of this they grow more obstinate, and hold their iniquities the faster, and that under the very hand of God, and his awful judgments that are on them, when he said surely they will receive instruction, and presumed that in their affliction they would seek him early, what is this but to stout it out against God; and that must necessarily be a very ill-boding symptom. This is the fearful brand which God himself sets on Ahaz in 2 Chron. 28:22, "And in the time of his distress did he yet trespass more against the Lord;" this is that king Ahaz. God is very angry when it is so, and declares against it, as that which highly provokes him. He therefore so articulates against them in Jer. 2:30, "In vain have I smitten your children, they received no correction." And it provokes him to give over correcting them and take a more awful course with

them; to lay by the rod, and to take the sword into his hand. To turn castigatory punishments into vindictive; hear that in Isa. 1:5, "Why will you be smitten any more? Ye will revolt more and more." In other words, you grow worse and worse under all the disciplinary means that are used with you, it is therefore high time to give them over, and take another way. There is nothing now but desolation that remains. All the endeavors that are used for reformation prove unsuccessful. It is sometimes so, that there is balm in Gilead, and a physician there, and yet there is no good done for it. There are those among a professing people who *do* zealously set themselves against the sins of the times and places they live in, and would gladly be instrumental, if it might be, of promoting a sincere and thorough reformation among their people, but all their most prudent and vigilant endeavors fail and are lost. The same iniquities abide, and raise up in the midst of them. Synods may be solemnly convened, provoking evils diligently sought out, suitable remedies faithfully prescribed, wholesome laws prudently enacted, churches be called on to, and engaged in the renewal of the covenant, and after all this, nothing may be amended; or if the wound be a little skinned over for a while, it breaks out again presently, and more fearfully. It was in this way with the kingdom of Judah in the times of Joash, as is fully recorded in 2 Chron. 24. Yes, and how much better was it in the times of that excellent Josiah? We may read the complaint that God makes against them, in the book of Zephaniah, and that threatening denounced in 1:12-13. And what indeed is there in such a case to be expected, but that God should cause his wrath to fall on such a people.

4. If rulers are left to do things which are greatly provoking to God, *delirant reges, plectuntur activi*. The error of rulers in their places are accustomed to have awful influences on the condition of that people over whom they are set; and the gross mistakes of these will make all to suffer. For they are public people, and the representatives of their people. If Saul in his zeal thinks that the Gibeonites ought to be cut off, because they were among the number of the once devoted people, and we know that the former judges had erred in their suffering of them, and for that reason had been for so many ages afflicted, and on this attempt, a three year famine is procured to the land by it, 2 Sam. 21:1ff, then yes, good and wise men have been sometimes left by God when he has been angry with a people. And by this it is to procure more judgments for them, as it was in David's case, 2 Sam. 24:1, "the anger of the Lord was kindled against Israel and he moved David to say, go number the people."

5. If a spirit of division is gotten among a people. Often, when the hand of God is heavy on them, instead of joining heart and hand in seeking after a redress of those things which God is provoked by, they fall into dissentions. In this there are divided judgments and divided hearts among them, so that they study and endeavor to thwart one another, and to impede each other in all attempts for good. On this nothing can go forward, but all things are put under an unavoidable check; this carries a very ill omen in it. It is in itself a

great punishment, and tending to many mischievous events that will naturally arise from it. Some good interpreters so understand that in Hosea 10:2, "Their heart is divided; now shall they be found faulty." It is indeed a terrible thing, for a people to be left to such a frame, that when providences call for unanimous endeavors in averting the wrath of God and their safety mainly depends on their unity, they expose themselves to become a prey, by their divisions, (Isa. 9:21).

6. If God's faithful messengers are despised, and their advice is trampled on. It has been a usual thing for God to stir up his servants in the ministry, to bear their testimony at such times, to declare against them the sins which are prevailing, and by which God's displeasure has been stirred up; and to give counsels and warnings to his people, both public and private; and it belongs to their office so to do, and God's warrant will bear them out in it. But if they are scorned, and their counsels are disregarded, and they themselves are censured as those that meddle with that which they have nothing to do with, it is an ill sign. Such a people shall know before God has done this as he did with the prophets. Asa is angry and enraged at the prophet who brought him a message from God, but it occasioned him more trouble, (2 Chron. 16). Amaziah bids the prophet who came to reprove him for his idolatry, to meddle with own business, and not to talk to him; but what follows? 2 Chron. 25:16, "I know, that God has determined to destroy thee, because thou hast done this, and hast not hearkened unto my counsel." Elijah is counted by Ahab to be the troubler of Israel because he bore a faithful

testimony against Israel's sins. And Jeremiah is voted to be a man of death, for his serious warnings and admonitions, but these were fearful presages of growing calamities, and were accordingly followed with it. God will be deeply provoked at such things, and answerable fruits are to be expected. These are some of those rules that are to be made use of in judging of the times. And the application belongs to everyone to make according as they are concerned.

FINIS

Reformation, the Great Duty of an Afflicted People

To the Reader[5]

Christian Reader,

How many ways God's hand is out against this people, and that he has now for a long time been managing a controversy with us, in a course of awful afflictive providences, is obvious to him who is not willingly a stranger in our Israel. We have tried many ways for the removal of our troubles, and, among others have kept many fasts, both public and private, to seek an atonement, and obtain help from heaven. Many also, if not the most of our churches have with solemnity revived their covenant obligations to God. But that after all our essays on this account, our distresses abide on us, and our perplexities are growing upon us, and God seems to blast our enterprises, to return our prayers with anger on us, to hide counsel, and take away our spirits from us. Yes, it seems he is exposing us to the scorn of our enemies, the language of the providences we

---

[5] Setting forth the sin and danger there is in neglecting of it, under the continued and repeated judgments of God. Being the substance of what was preached on a solemn day of humiliation kept by the third gathered church in Boston, on August 23rd 1694. By Samuel Willard, teacher of the said church. Zech. 1:3, "Thus saith the Lord of hosts, turn unto me saith the Lord of hosts, and I will turn unto you saith the Lord of hosts." (Boston, MA: Bartholomew Green, 1694).

are now under speaks plainly. And what may be the meaning of these things? We are by name and profession a people of God; and there are great promises made to such, in case of their close walking with God. Yes, and though they have sinned, and brought troubles on themselves, if they truly repent, they can return to him. Without a doubt, if God had not been angry, we would have not been so afflicted; and if he had not been provoked by our sins, he would not have been angry; and if we had hearkened to the voice of the rod, it would have been removed, and not continued, and harder strokes would not have been inflicted. That which God expects of us is *reformation*; and though this belongs to each of us personally; and if everyone would take heed to himself, and mend one, the whole would be amended. There is a common concern lying on us, as we are a people whose interests are bound up together; so God treats us in his providence as a community. It is without a doubt, then, that it is not likely to become better with us as a people, until such a reformation is promoted; and there are the measures and steps to be taken in it, which, it is to be feared, have now been neglected. What these are the scriptures will inform us, and the examples of God's people recorded in them, stands for our direction in this affair.

  The design of the following discourse was only to show the necessity of this duty, and to stimulate all that heard it, to do what is in their scope towards the furtherance of such a work. God is signifying to us, that nothing else will make him content; and he is yet in the way of his judgments, both giving us opportunity to attend it, and loudly calling upon us so to do. And if this word added to the other manifest speakings of our God to us, may contribute to awakening this people to a serious settling about this duty, and a vigorous pursuance of it, God shall have the praise. It made, through mercy, some impression on the hearts of many hearers; if this publication may be blessed to fixing it on such, and to the rousing of others, that we may be a truly reforming people, and God may turn from his anger, it will be found a word spoken in season; to God's gracious blessing I commend it, who am,

The least and most unworthy of ministers,
SAMUEL WILLARD.

Reformation the great duty of an afflicted people.

Leviticus 26:23, "If ye will not be reformed by me by these things, but will walk contrary unto me, then will I also walk contrary unto you, and will punish you yet seven times for your sins."

In this chapter, from verse 3, after that God had, by Moses given to the people of Israel the several statutes and judgments, where he required their cordial obedience, he declares to them the terms of the covenant between him and them, as he afterwards did in the same manner n the rehearsal of the law a little before Moses' death, (Deut. 28). This is the same for its substance with this, though they are spoken in words diversely expressed. In it there are three parts contained. 1. A declaration of those blessings which God engaged to their obedience, to verse 14. 2. A menace of such judgments as they should be visited with in case of their disobedience and obstinacy, to verse 40. 3. A promise made to them of mercy, and restoration, on their repentance after all of it, to verse 46. He is more brief in the account given of the first and last of these, but commemorates more largely upon the second.

Before I come to a more particular explanation on this matter, it will be requisite that I remove an objection out of the way; *viz.*, it may be, and it is said by some, that these terms here proposed are *legal*, and therefore not proper to be applied to us in gospel times, who are under *another* covenant, and treated by God with other manner of dispensations towards us. To which let me briefly reply. There were many and great differences in the manner of God's dispensing of himself to his people before and after the coming of Christ in the flesh. On this account of this diversity it was once called the old covenant, and the one in Christ the new one. The former is suited to the childish, the latter to the virile age of the church, as the apostle illustrates it in, Galatians 4:1. Among which, this was one that God then treated them more with terrors, and now in the new covenant more with promises, children needing more of severity to be used with them, than such as are grown to years of a riper understanding. Where the moral law was revived on Mount Sinai with thunderings and lightnings, and amazing terrors, which put a consternation into the people; and Moses is usually more explanative in the minatory than the promissory part of the covenant. God also then more insisted on the external considerations of temporary favors and afflictions, where in the gospel such as are spiritual are more inculcated. Yet, the covenant which God entered into with his people then, and that which he makes with us in the days of the gospel, is, for the substance; *one and the same.* All the covenants which ever God made with men, are reducible to one of these two, *viz.*, either the covenant of works, or the covenant of grace. And it is certain, that whatever transaction there has been in a covenant way between God and man since Adam's apostasy, is of grace, that of works being by the fall, made unable any more to give life to man, (Gal. 3:21). And here, though the moral law was renewed with this people, and solemnly proclaimed to them, yet it was given in the hands of a mediator, (Gal.

3:19). And it is to be observed, that God's public transactions with any people, considered as they are a body, referring to mercies and judgments, are restrained to this life and world. The future judgment of the Great Day shall not be of communities as such, for there will then be an end of them, but everyone there and then must personally answer for himself. But here there are both temporal and spiritual mercies and miseries, blessings and curses to be dispensed unto such according to their behavior. We read that godliness has the promise of the life that now is, (1 Tim. 4:8). And that God's people are judged in this world, (1 Cor. 11). The judgments therefore which befell the church in the wilderness, are proposed to our consideration as exemplary to us, and we are advised to take warning by them, that we may escape suffering in the same way, (1 Cor. 10:11).

These things being thus premised, let us take a more particular view of the matter before us and here, (1.) It is supposed that a people in this way circumstanced may prevaricate; they may neglect to pay their due obedience to God which he requires of them, no, they may despise the commands of God, and turn their backs on them, (verses 14-15). For this is the hypothesis on which the threatening is built. And if it were not a thing possible, and that of which there was at least some danger, the threatening would be needless, and it is very obvious that sometimes a people that make a great pretense to religion, will dare in this way to do, and that notwithstanding the threatening stands as a thorn hedge to keep them in. They will adventure on it, although they scratch themselves on the thorns.

(2.) God threatens to bring awful judgments upon them in case they do so transgress, (verses 16-17). Their covenant relation, and their nearness to God by reason of it, shall be no security to them against the miseries mentioned. Sin will break down this hedge, and let the wild beasts upon them, to devour them.

(3.) It is further presumed that these judgments will not amend them, but that they will persist in their apostasy, and proceed yet to *greater* revolts. And this is supposed from one step to another, unto every one of which there is menaced a process in the way of judgments, and an augmentation of their miseries, until they come to the height. And this is mentioned four times, one of which is in our text, of which we may, at present make some improvement for our instruction.

The words are very emphatic. I might observe the various manner of expressing this, which is used in the four several instances; but I shall supersede that. In our text is contained a hypothetical commination, in which observe, 1. The hypothesis itself, verse 23. And that is, that the judgments which have been inflicted on them, do not reform them; they are not reclaimed by them; *i.e.* they remain still obstinate, in which there are several things to be noted. 1]. It is supposed that they have before sinned against the covenant, so as to bring the judgments of God on themselves. They are looked on as a people under the effects of divine displeasure for their sins. 2]. It is presumed that these judgments so brought on them have not obtained the proper end which was expected by them; where we have the aim or end pointed at, *viz.*, to reform them. 3]. It is looked on to be after such time as God has been more than once trying of them in this way, and yet it has not taken effect, or proved successful. The instance in our text, is the third case mentioned, after the first trial had not succeeded. 4]. The nature of this impenitence is expressed in the hypothesis. 1). Negatively; if ye be not reformed. 2). Positively; but walk contrary unto me.

2. Here is the consequent threatening in case such be the event of former trials, verse 24. Where is pointed, 1). The manner of his carriage towards them, *I will walk contrary to you.* 2). The aggravation of the punishment, *and will punish you yet seven times for your sins.* I shall not here tarry to criticize upon the words; if there is any occasion it may be remarked in the sequel. There are several great practical truths, suitable for the present occasion, which may be taken up from the words, and briefly improved.

DOCTRINE 1:
The great design of all God's judgments on a professing people is to reform them.

The word signifies *to bind*, and metaphorically *to chasten*, and then metonymically, to *reform or reclaim*, that being its desirable genuine effect; and so it must be here understood. When I say this is the design, I do not speak of the end of the purpose which is secret, but of the precept which requires it, and of the providence, which is said to speak about it. This then is the revealed and proposed end. This may be opened and cleared in a few things.

1. That public calamities may be the lot of a professing people to meet with. This needs no proof, in being so manifestly exemplified in the providence of God, in all the ages of the church, that we may as well question the suns shining at noon day in a clear sky. The true emblem of the militant church is a bush on fire. Such a people are obnoxious to God, to devils, and to wicked men, and there are occasions for expecting them to meet with trouble from them all.

2. That usually they procure these afflictions to themselves by some apostasy. God may indeed exercise them for the trial of their obedience, and sincerity in it. Afflictions which are merely probationary are not only suffered personally, but may be publicly too; did not God do so by the kingdom of Judah under Hezekiah, in the time of a most zealous and thorough reformation? And there is an astonishment put on it, (2 Chron. 32:1ff). "After these things, and the establishment thereof," *etc.* But, though God sometimes, for holy ends, in this way uses his sovereignty, for the most part there has some great provocation or other gone before, which procured these troubles for them. And this is very agreeable to the tenor of the covenant, in which God has engaged to bestow his favors on a people, that walk before him in the truth, and therefore the apostle has such a challenge, 1 Peter 3:13, "Who is he that will harm you, if you be followers of that which is good?" And God himself in this way expostulates with his people, when they were

suffering his judgments, Jer. 2:17, "Hast thou not procured this to thyself, in that thou hast forsaken the Lord thy God?"

3. That here these judgments are God's testimony that he bears against that sin. And they are the discoveries which he makes of the displeasure that he takes at it. They are the tokens of his anger by which he gives them to understand how ill he resents it that they have broken his laws, and gone back from his command. These therefore are, in scripture language, called his anger, his wrath, his displeasure; because they are the discoveries of it. When he brings them on men, they feel those things which speaks about him as offended at them. They are such things as are accustomed in men to proceed from such a passion; and are ascribed to him after the manner of men, in whom are no passions properly so called.

4. They are of the discipline which God, by covenant, engages to exercise towards his people. It is therefore one article mentioned in the covenant on this hypothesis, Psalm 89:30, *etc.* "If his children forsake my law," *etc.* "Then will I visit their transgressions with the rod, and their iniquity with stripes." And the apostle expresses it as so, Heb. 12:6, "He scourgeth every son whom be receiveth," *i.e.,* "he receiveth" him on such terms. It is therefore called a rod, which is used for discipline, and not for ruin. They are called *corrections*, which, though they have anger in them, and suppose a fault which procures them, is yet tempered with love which manages the anger for good. And always,

correction is administered for reformation of the party that undergoes it.

5. These judgments are to be annumerated to the long-suffering which God uses towards a sinning people. This therefore is attributed to him and is to be read in these dispensations. As he waits before he smites them, so he waits in smiting of them, and what is this for, but to see for their amendment if it may in this way be obtained? Consider then, Hosea 5:15, "I will go," *etc.* "In their affliction they will seek me early." And indeed, there is a great deal of mercy in it; God corrects when he might cut off; he afflicts instead of destroying, which they deserved, and might have suffered, if he had strained the advantage offered him. This is the church's acknowledgment, Lam. 3:22, "it is of the Lord's mercy that we are not consumed." And so the good man in Nehemiah 9:31, "For thy great mercies sake, thou didst not utterly consume them."

6. God is accustomed, with these judgments, to send them invitations to repentance, and offers of his favors if they repent. This is a privilege that a people in covenant with God enjoy, that not only does he warn and advise them before he strikes, so that, if it might be, blows might be prevented, but while he is striking them as well. He calls on them now to consider their ways, Haggai 1:5, "Whiles they are under afflictions." He tells them that he does not thirst for their blood, or seek opportunities to ruin them; but would have them to turn that they may prevent it, and he declares it solemnly. Ezekiel 33:11, "As I live, I delight not in the death," *etc.* "Turn ye, turn ye, why will ye die, Oh house of Israel?"

And he declares that if they do turn he will receive them, and turn his anger away from them Jer. 3:22, "Return ye backsliding children, and I will heal your backslidings;" and so chapter 4:1.

7. God has been accustomed, on their reformation, to avert his judgments from his people. This is a course that has not failed. How often did he do so for his people of old! As we shall find on record in biblical history. No, such has been the pity which he has extended to them in this regard, that when their reformation has been feigned, and not upright, yet he has delivered them out of everything, and that many a time, as is intimated in Psalm 78:34. How much more then will he do so when it is hearty, and sincere? It is a very remarkable passage in Judges 10:15-16.

8. Therefore, the reason why God has at any time proceeded to extirpate a professing people has been their impenitence. When neither word nor rod, neither warnings nor judgments would prevail with them to return, but they have remained obstinate under all; see an account of this, 2 Chron. 36:15-16, he waited until there was no remedy; no other course to be taken. All their other provocations, though never so many and heinous, would never have brought it to this, if they had not added contumacy to their apostasy; Therefore, we have God using of that expostulation with them, (Isaiah 48:18-19).

Use 1. Learn from this, that if a professing people perish at last, they must blame themselves. Well might God say to them as he did, Hosea 13:9, "Oh Israel! Thou hast destroyed thyself." All the sore judgments and calamities, which God brings on a sinning people, are not in themselves any symptom of their ruin; are not a sure token that God has forsaken them; though sometimes sinners, when sorely visited, they are ready to say, "my God has forgotten me." But on the other hand, there is an argument that God is loath to destroy them, and therefore he first tries whether by such judgments this may not be prevented. What the apostle says in, 1 Cor. 11:32, "When we are judged, we are chastened of the Lord, that we should not be condemned with the world," is applicable here. God by afflicting of a sinful people, shows that he would not destroy them, unless they themselves are resolved in their own destruction. There is a voice in the rod, and he would have them to hear it, and him who has appointed it, (Micah 6:9). And he has more than once said it, that if they will hear it shall be well with them for all. If then they will not hear, but stop their ears at this voice, and harden their hearts against the advice of it, and so they perish, where is the fault?

Use 2. Let this then serve to point us to our present duty. It tells us what it is that is now incumbent on us. We are a people whom God has taken near to himself, who have been privileged with his covenant favors and blessings; whom he has done many and great things for. But he has signally altered the course of his providence towards us and brought us under his rod; his hand is many ways out against us, and we are made low. He has wasted us by striking us many ways, and we are reduced to great distresses. And what is all this for but our iniquities? If we had not revolted from him, he would not have afflicted us. Our peace, and our prosperity might have continued uninterrupted, and he would have delighted in it. What then remains, but that we set on a real and a thorough reformation? And let us be serious in it. Are there not the things among us that need reforming? Is there not a fearful decay of love, and zeal, and holiness among us? Is not almost everything that can be thought of out of order among us? And is our God now manifesting of the dislike that he takes at it? What have we to do then, but to set on this work in good earnest? Let all orders of men be invited to it. Let us all search, and try, and turn, (Lam. 3:40). And to move us to this, *consider:*

1. God is waiting to be gracious. Whatever displays he gives us of his righteous anger, and they are awful, yet still he is to be sought in the way of his judgments, (Isa. 26:8). Though he is scourging of us by his afflictive providences, yet he is still hearkening to hear if there be any inclination in us this way; if there is the least motions or stirrings in our hearts towards it; and he will take it well of us if there is; he therefore makes that complaint on this account, Jer. 8:6, "I hearkened and heard, but none spake aright," *etc.*

2. Listen, if we do reform, there is hope. May we not say as he did in Ezra 10:2-3, "We have trespassed against our God, yet now there is hope in Israel concerning this thing, now therefore let us make a covenant with our God." And observe what great encouragement there is given for our so doing, Joel 2:12, *etc.* "God is merciful and gracious, and ready to repent of the evil, and he has his end in smiting of us." If this may but be obtained, the design of corrective providences is

fully answered, and so the controversy is ended when once it arrives at this. Why then do we sit still? Why do we pine away in our iniquities because we do not put them away from us? Let us be up and doing, and the Lord will accept of us.

DOCTRINE 2:
A declined professing people, may meet with sore judgments, and yet remain unreformed under and after them.

This is supposed and presumed in our text, and remember, it is the fourth step in the process of God's judicial dispensation towards them; and we are not to think such things are here supposed which may not be. We shall therefore find awful instances of this truth on record in the word of God, giving us to understand that it has been so as stated in my *thesis*. What great pains did God afterwards take with this people for their reformation, when they had forgotten the works that he had done in Egypt, and in the wilderness, and were revolted from him? And yet what was the issue he had in all this? Although he sent all his servants the prophets to them, rising up early and sending them, by whom he laid evident convictions of their sins, before them, gave them awful warnings of his impending judgments, and urged on them solemn and serious invitations to repent, with the fairest promises of his favor in case of their compliance with it. And though he laid many and severe strokes on them, bringing of them low for their iniquities, wasting them in every way, yet to what purpose was it? What effect did it work in them? We are told, that God would have purged them, but they were not purged; this is the complaint that is made against them in Ezek. 24:13. "They held fast their deceit, and would not let it go." So it went on. "Why then is this people of Jerusalem slidden back by a perpetual backsliding? they hold fast deceit, they refuse to return," (Jer. 8:5). Nor is this at all to be wondered at, if we shall consider the *following:*

    1. The body of a professing people are not always truly gracious. To be sure, in times in which there is a decay of holiness, and increase of impiety, it is not likely to be so. All are not Israel that are of Israel. There is indeed a bored ear in the children of God, that inclines them to be ready to hearken to the voice of the rod, and to be awakened to discipline; to be of a tender heart, and resent the displeasure of God; this is the natural and genuine working of grace in the heart wherein it is really planted. But all are not so who are the people of God by external denomination, and a verbal profession. When apostasy begins to creep on a people, conversion work begins to be more rare, and men are not so frequently brought home to God by a thorough and saving change worked in them. Hypocrisy and luke-warmness begin to get ahead and prevail, and the power of godliness ceases, and men rest contented in a name to live while they are dead. We have the character of such a church fully represented to us in that of Laodicea, in Rev. 3:14, *etc.* And it is not seldom exemplified in the world, where the name of Christ is taken up.

2. God's own children are sometimes judicially left under obstinate frames. It is the mournful expostulation of the church, Isa. 63:17, "O Lord, why hast thou made us to err from thy ways, and hardened our hearts from thy fear?" And though there is a principle of saving grace in them, which inclines them to a holy fear, yet they have a body of death too, which has it influence on them, and that so powerful, that they are drawn by it into the sins of the times and places they live in, and God is displeased at them for it, and so he awfully leaves them to have their ears stopped, so as not to give ear, as they ought to do, to the warnings he gives, and the judgments which he inflicts. We have instances for this in Eli, David, Asa, serving to let us understand, how far holy men may, under desertion, provoke their father to displeasure, and thereby open away for more temporal judgments to come on them.

3. Natural men have no true liking to the ways of God. They are in their sins, and so their hearts are set for sin. Lust has dominion in them, and all the powers of their souls are engaged for it; their understanding approves it, it calls evil good; their wills give it the preference, and so makes choice of it, and their affections are set on it. On this, their close keeping to duty, and their abstinence from sin is a forced thing, and against the whole bent of their natures; it is a yoke that does not sit easy on their necks, but feels very irksome to them. And this makes them in a readiness to shake it off, and glad of an opportunity so to do; and such opportunities, the times of declension afford enough of to them. When many sins grow common, and not so scandalous, and

witness begins not to be born against them as sometimes it had been, now the before hidden corruption looks forth and shows its head. And when once they are gotten into such a way, they are willing to hold it fast, and do not care for being disturbed in it, or turning away from it. There is that complaint, Jer. 5:23, "This people has a revolting and rebellious heart, they are revolted and gone."

  4. Afflictions, or judgments do not have in themselves the virtue of reforming a backslidden people. They are indeed made use of by God for this purpose, and if he pleases to influence them, they shall be serviceable to its furtherance, and suitable moral arguments may be drawn from them for conviction and awakening. But they cannot alone work any gracious effect. Unless correction and instruction go together, there is no good likely to be done. Hear Psalm 94:12, "Blessed is the man whom thou chastenest, O Lord, and teachest him out of thy law," otherwise, "bray a fool in a mortar among wheat with a pestle, yet will not his foolishness depart from him," (Prov. 27:22). Men might indeed know, if they would, what afflictions come for, and that would be a step to reformation, if there were a thorough conviction on the conscience; but there is no kindly working on the heart by this alone. Unsanctified afflictions, being mis-improved by the native corruption that is in man, will make him worse, and more obstinate, instead of mending him; 2 Chron. 28:22, "And in the time of his distress he did yet trespass more against the Lord."

5. Sinful men are hard to be persuaded to believe that they are the guilty causes of the judgments that are on God's people. Men indeed are apt at such times to make a fearful cry against sin, talk much of the provocation that is given to God, as if they had a mind to find it out and have it removed. But yet, everyone is apt to put it off from himself and lay it on others. There is a great deal of noise made at such a time, but what is there in it? If we observe we shall find that it is only throwing dirt one on another; but as for themselves, they are clear and innocent. They have nothing to accuse themselves of. If others would have been as careful as they, this might have been avoided. How does God make such a complaint as this? Jer. 8:6, "I hearkened and heard, but they spake not aright. No man repented him of his wickedness, saying what have I done?" There is such a drunkenness in men, that they cannot think their ways are perverse, they can see no evil in them, so are they charged, Isa. 44:20, "A deceived heart has turned him aside, that he cannot deliver his own soul, nor say, is there not a lie in my right hand?"

6. Therefore, until God pours out his Spirit on them, men remain in this way stupid and senseless. There must be an inward working on the hearts of men by the Spirit of God, if ever they are by his judgments worked up to reformation. Until he gives them eyes to see, and hearts to consider, they continue as foolish as ever. Let one judgment come on them in the neck of another, let them be broken, wasted, consumed, and almost laid desolate, and they are obdurate still; all this will not melt down their hard hearts, or bring them to

any kindly compliance with God. It is an observation made by the prophet, Isa. 42:25, "Therefore he has poured on him the fury of his anger, and the strength of battle. And it has set him on fire round about, yet he knew it not; and it burned him, yet he laid it not to heart."

Use 1. Learn from this, that judgments alone, are not a sure sign that God has a purpose of good for such a people as suffer by them. It is true, they do bear witness for God, that he is very loath to destroy them, if it might in any other way be prevented. They say that he is a God of great patience, and that he is waiting for the repentance of such a people, so that he may yet be favorable to them and establish them. Otherwise he could as easily have cut them off at a stroke and must have been justified in his doing so. But still, we can make no certain judgment of the issue, until we see what influence and efficacy these judgments have on them; the conclusion is still suspended. If once they appear to work kindly, and begin to awaken them to enquire into the provocation, and seriously to set about the work of reformation, there is then a good hope offered us, that all will end well at last.

But if still they do not reform, no, if reiterated judgments do not produce such an effect as this is on them, but they still persist in their evil ways, and are rather hardened in them by these afflictions, there is abundant reason given us to be very doubtful what it will come to at the last.

Use 2. Let it then put us on the enquiry, what effect all the strokes of God which we have felt, have worked on us. And it is of no small consequence that we do in good earnest make this enquiry, as will more evidently appear in the following observations. That we have been under the discipline of God's judgments is not to be called into question; let us then see to it what is the fruit of everything from it on us. We are here given to understand that all so treated are not reformed; and it is not everything that looks fair, which will amount to the reformation which God expects. It is not crying out of sin in general, nor calling of solemn assemblies, fasting, praying, confessing, petitioning, renewing of covenants, making of laws, putting away of some more gross and enormous sins that are apparently provoking, that will answer God's expectation, and so put a stop to his anger, and turn away his judgments from us. It is another manner thing altogether, though, to reform. Let us then be very inquisitive into his matter, and make a diligent search about it. If we think that we have done it, or are in the way to the doing of it, when there is no such thing, we shall miserably deceive ourselves; and it will be no little damage that will arise to us from it. And one would think that a small enquiry on this account, would be sufficient both to convince and condemn us. There has been so much of notorious flightiness and neglect in this regard, that it is hard to say what one thing has been amended. And if we shall call all that we have here been doing, a reformation, will not God upbraidingly say to us, "is this the reformation that I have required? Is this the point that you have made so much concern of and about? Is this all that you intend?"

DOCTRINE 3:
If God's judgments do not reform a backslidden people, the blame lies in their willfulness.

Here the Lord charges it, not "if" you "do not," but "if ye will not reform." All the impenitency of a backslidden people is the effect of their obstinacy. This is not to be understood so, as if they did not labor of impotency in themselves, or as if they had a power in themselves to reform themselves, which is the mistaken inference which some draw from such scriptures as charge sin on man's willfulness. No, it must be granted that they cannot reform themselves; although it is also certain that externally, or with respect to practice, they might do a great deal more than they do; and that will manifestly declare them as inexcusable. But truly to turn from sin, and cordially to return to God from whom they have departed, is a work above their ability, and the Spirit of God must powerfully work it in them, if ever it is done. But still God is accustomed to lay the blame of their not being reformed, not on their impotency, but their willfulness. Thus Matthew 23:37, "How often would I have gathered thy children, but ye would not." John 5:40, "Ye will not come unto me," and here lies the height of its wickedness; and that it is so, will be made to appear, if we consider these three things.

1. That a principal part of the natural impotency of men, lies in the depravity of their wills. It is true, man's

whole nature and all the faculties in him are debilitated, sin having a rooting in them all, and robbed them of the image of God, by which once man was fitted with ability for his work; but as the will is the leading faculty in the man, so is the impotency of it very notorious. That sin which men are full of, has laid fast hold on them, and engaged their hearts to it, and they have made choice of it, and that according to the dictates of a depraved understanding. For that being filled with crooked principles, causing it to judge perversely of things, and quite contrary to what they are in reality, has drawn away the will after it, into a spontaneous and deliberate election and embracement of these delusions; and that it is by their will that men hold fast deceit, (Jer. 8:5). Their sins have so gained not only their approbation, to prefer them before holiness, but also their affections; they love the ways of iniquity, and that makes them to adhere to them. Jer. 2:25, "I have loved strangers, and after them I will go." And by this their wills are become so impotent, that they cannot make a better choice of themselves, or by their own power. And yet all this is voluntary; there is no outward force laid on them to cause them to do this, but it is a fruit of the native corruption which is in them.

    2. That men do willfully shut their eyes against the convictions which are laid before them, by which they might be led to reformation. The afflictions themselves which they suffer, are for conviction; there is such a design in them, God sends them for sin, and they are to bring it to remembrance. They have a voice in them, and it is intelligible. They say that God is angry

with such a people, and they serve to put men on enquiry after the cause of them. Even the Philistines themselves are led by the light of nature to ask such a question when the hand of God is on them, acknowledging that it was from him, and on this to consult how they might obtain a removal of it, (1 Sam. 6:1ff). Yes, and many times the judgments bring light in and with them, to discover the ground of the controversy, and point to the very sin against which they are witnesses. Adonibezek was in this way brought to a confession of his cruelty, and God's just vindication, (Judges 1:7). But besides this, when God comes to punish a people that are in covenant with him, he is accustomed, together with these troubles, to send them matter of conviction in his ordinances, to awaken his servants in the ministry, to touch their hearts, and suggest to them the things that he contends for, and make them to cry aloud and not to spare, but to show his people the sins they are guilty of; and to do it with all evidence and demonstration. He does this so that if men would but listen and give ear to these cries and convictions, they might be thoroughly convinced and not be able to withstand. But the reason why they do not do this, is because they will not. What they said brazenly to the prophet, Jer. 44:16, "As for the word that thou hast spoken to us in the name of the Lord, we will not hearken unto thee." These say the same practically, which amounts to as much in the event, and is so interpreted by God as if their tongues had uttered it. And this is to be charged on all that do not take the warnings, and bring themselves to the light of the truth, that they may know their sins. And what is the reason why they will not readily receive the light, but shut their eyes against it, and do what in them lies to keep it out? It is because they are resolved to hold on their sinful courses, and would be quiet in it; which that they may, they would prevent the reflections of conscience, which is most likely done by keeping them in the dark. Our Savior tells us how it is, and why it is so in this regard, John 3:19-20. Men's ways "are evil," and they are afraid to know that they are so, and to be reproved for them; they therefore resolve to resist all the means that might bring them to a knowledge of themselves and their evil doings.

    3. That men will not receive the help which otherwise they might have, to remove all the other impediments of their reformation. It is true, none can turn themselves, until God puts in his grace and turns them, he must first draw us, before we can run after him. It was a right prayer which Ephraim put up, Jer. 31:18ff, "Turn thou me, and I shall be turned." But God, in his ordinances, offers to his people, together with reproofs, all the assistance and grace that is lacking to do of that which he requires of them. He uses all means and endeavors with them, tendering them his hand, but they reject him. They will have none of him, they had rather go without his help; they are not willing to be rid of their sins. They are therefore said to resist his spirit; and on this, the reason rendered why God at length leaves them up to their sinful ways, and gives them over to their vile courses to sin without any restraints, is because they would not accept of these his gracious offers. Psalm

81:11-12, "My people would not hearken to my voice," *etc.* "So I gave them up to their own heart's lust," *etc.*

Use 1. Learn from this, how inexcusable we shall be, if under all God's judgments we do not reform. Men are ready to think they have a great deal to plead for themselves by way of excuse. Alas! If God does not give them grace to repent and reform, how should they ever do it? They have no power of themselves, and if they should attempt it, what would it turn to? If therefore they lie in their sins, and pine away in their iniquities, how can they help it? This seems to be the meaning of their language in Ezek. 33:10. But this will not stand men in any stead. If indeed men had a heart to it, and a desire after it, if they were really for it, and used cordial endeavors after it, if they did truly bewail this impotency of theirs, and cry out importunately and heartily to God for his help against it, as those that were weary of their sins, and would gladly be rid of them, and God should refuse them his grace, and withhold this necessary help from them, something then might be pleaded. But when was it ever this way? When did God withhold his grace from such as did indeed desire it, and ask for it? He has promised, and always practiced the contrary. No, no, the will is in it, we are set against it, we have chosen our own ways. They best please us. We cannot part with them. God calls us once and again, and he strikes us at one time and another, and we stop our ears at him, turn our backs on him, shut our eyes, and harden our hearts. And what can such a people say for themselves, against whom it will be proved that they were willfully set in their own way, in despite of all courses used to reclaim them.

Whoever excused such as willfully transgressed this is that which all man's reason accounts a consideration that takes away all excuse.

Use 2. Let this then serve to convince and humble us in this regard, and doubtless we have great occasion for it. Has not God been using all manner of endeavors with us, to bring us to a sight and sense of our sins, and to make us know that it is an evil and a bitter thing that we have forsaken him to such a degree as we have, and that feelingly by the sense of all those sharp strokes that he has laid on us. And there have been many of them, and no little of his severity exercised in them. And has he not in the meanwhile been sending as many faithful warnings, clear convictions, and awakening loud calls in his house and ordinances, and that from time to time? Have not all his servants been unanimously engaged in this design? Has there been anything wanting as to means? What more could he have done, than what he has done? No, have we not been convinced in our consciences, and enforced by them to make confessions on this account? Has he not also kindly invited us to lay hold on his strength, and be at peace with him? Offering us all fair terms in the treaty he has been holding all this while with us? What is the reason then that there is no more reformation worked in our midst? Have we been willing, and God unwilling? He will certainly make us to know that there is no such matter until he has finished with us. How then should this confound us, and lay us in the dust before him? How should it fill us with shame, and clothe us in sackcloth? Let us then see and confess the naughtiness of our own hearts; and take the blame home to ourselves. Let us acknowledge as Ephraim, Jer. 31:18, "We have been as a bullock unaccustomed to the yoke." This is the great complaint which we have at this day to make of ourselves before God, and bitterly to bewail it in his presence, that we have hardened our hearts against him. That we have obstinately set ourselves to withstand all the attempts which he has been using to reclaim us. And let us be no more stiff necked, but bring these hard hearts of ours to him to have them made tender, and beg of him to take the stone out of them, and work them to a true compliance with his will; that we may have a true resentment of all his judgments and be humbled under them. And if this may be obtained, we are in a fair way to be reformed; and then there will be a good hope that he will return and save us. And what a happy day would this prove for us, if it might come to this issue?

DOCTRINE 4:
An unreformed professing people do all the while walk contrary to God.

In this way he interprets it in the text. This is the very sense that he puts on it; in the Hebrew it is, "shall walk with me contrarily." And the manner of expression seems to have something observable in it, noting a pretense of being his people, and making it their design to walk with him, *i.e.* in conformity to his commands; and yet a carrying of it contrary, to the pretense of their practice. And the phrase notes an opposition, or a setting of themselves against God. And that such a people as do not, will not reform, do in this way, will appear on the consideration of these things.

1. All apostasy is a revolting from God. A people that are in covenant with him, have acknowledged and submitted to his sovereignty over them. They have owned him to be their Lord, and their king, and their Law-giver and bound themselves to yield obedience to all his commands; promised that all that the Lord shall speak to them, they will do it. Now God has given them his orders, according to which he expects that they should regulate themselves, and in this give a testimony of their loyalty to him. Every professing people are brought under this bond of the covenant when therefore they depart from his obedience, and turn aside to their crooked ways, they in this depart from their allegiance. Here it is called "a revolting," Jer. 5:23, "They are revolted, and gone." And the name of revolters is put on them, in Jeremiah 6:28, "They are all grievous" revolters. And what is this but a setting of themselves against him? A rebel is certainly, by his rebellion, set against his lawful duty.

2. In this apostasy, must necessarily be a maintaining of that contrariety. They fell into this way by their departure from him, and they walk on in it by their impenitency. By this they do, as it were, fortify themselves against him, strengthen themselves in their rebellion. Every new act of disobedience to his commands, is a renewed actual opposing of themselves to him; and by every such act they do as much as say, that they are resolved to withstand him. The life of man is compared to a walk, and every action that is done in it,

is a step in that walk; and so long as they are out of the right way, and still going, they do but increase their revolt. Every sinner is a rebel; he that persists in his sin, is a hardened rebel; and this must necessarily be a woeful contrariety to God. God is then only complied with when men do repent of their sins; for that is it which he requires of them; willful impenitence then is a setting of themselves to oppose this will of his; and what can be more contrary than this?

3. They do by this set themselves against all the attempts that God is using with them for the reclaiming of them. God always, when a people of his covenant begins to decline from his precepts, to apply things seasonably and suitably to them for their recovery, so that the breakings forth of his hot anger may be prevented. On this account he tells them of their declinings, invites them to return speedily, and not go on. He warns them of the danger they lay themselves open to, threatens them with his rods in case they do not hear him, yes, and when this is put to it, he strikes them with his judgments, and all this to recover them. But they do all they can to make void these attempts, and this is a woeful contrariety. Their neglecting to reform under such essays used with them, is to set themselves against all the pleadings of God, to quench all the motions and stirrings of the spirit in them, to withstand all the calls of the judgments that are on them, in which God cries aloud to them to return and to repent. In this way, they set their wills against his will; he says to them, "turn from your evil courses, amend your ways and your doings," but they do not, and that is in effect to say that

they will not, and this is the interpretation God puts on it. So, as much as they can, they look to make all the pains that God takes with them to be in vain; and what is this but to rebel against him and walk contrary?

4. By this they do provoke God to jealousy, and dare him to do his worst. In this way such a people are found to be fighters against him. They that will not be reformed by these things, do cast a great contempt on his judgments. This is interpretatively to despise them, and shows that such do presume. To be too hard for God at the last. We find what a sense God himself puts on it, Isa. 28:15, "Ye have said, we have made a covenant with death," *etc.,* "when the overflowing scourge shall pass through, it shall not come nigh us," *etc.* And we have the apostle in this way expostulating on the account, 1 Cor. 10:22, "Do we provoke the Lord to jealousy? Are we stronger than he?" God says that if they will not reform, he will heap his plagues on them, and multiply their calamities; and they say, their carriage speaks it, let him do it if he will, they are not concerned about it; they are purposed to run the adventure of it, and try whether he will do as he says. And what greater contrariety can there be than this? This is to *beat* a challenge to heaven, and run up against the thick bosses of his buckler. This shows that they are set against him; which must necessarily be a very bold and daring presumption.

5. And in this they withstand his glory and seek his dishonor. When men are affected with the tokens of his displeasure, and are brought to confess and forsake those sins which have procured it, and in this way address him for his pardon and favor, they do in this give

glory to God. This is to throw down their arms, and resign themselves to him, and he reckons himself to be honored by their so doing. But when they do willfully maintain their sins and will not kindly accept of the punishment of them, they do by this cast reproach on him. They do withstand the glory of his holiness, while they pretend to be his people, to have his name called on them, and yet they will live after the manner of the heathen. And for all that, presume that he who is a God of purer eyes than to behold iniquity, and cannot endure sin, should own them to be his, and favor them, and patronize their abominations, like them, Jer. 7:9, steal, murder, commit adultery *etc.* And come into this house, and say "we are delivered to do all these abominations." And if this is not to dishonor him, what can be? Moreover, they slight his power, in that they are not afraid to irritate him to exert it, briars and thorns so set themselves in battle against the devouring fire. They cast contempt on his justice, as if he would connive at such sins, and would not visit them for these things. They open the mouths of adversaries against him, who here take occasion to blaspheme his great name; and they slight his authority over them, while they withdraw their necks from under his yoke, and deny him the due obedience. And surely all this carries in it a horrible contrariety to him.

Use 1. We learn from this, how dangerous a thing it is to live and lie in any sin unrepented of. Does God put such an account on it? Does he reckon all such to walk contrary to him? Surely then it must stir up his anger and provoke him to wrath against them. It will kindle the fire of his fury, and make it to burn up into a fearful flame, and how terrible must this necessarily be? The apostle thought it so, Heb. 10:31, "It is a fearful thing to fall into the hands of the living God." Surely then it is a daring adventure of those that will expose themselves on this hazard, and, as it were, force him to take them in hand, and be revenged on them, and necessarily must it issue in the unspeakable misery of all those that will be so bold. Observe what a challenge God makes on this account, Isa. 27:4, "Who would set the briars and thorns against me in battle? I would go through them, I would burn them together," and so we may easily guess how it is likely to wind up. We have an account of the unhappy success that is like to come of such an unequal duel, Job 15:24-26, "Shall a potsherd of the earth strive with his maker, and hope to come off with anything less than ruin?"

Use 2. Let it then be an awakening word of warning to us. And we are not a little concerned in it. We have without a doubt fallen by our iniquity. We have gotten too far away from God; we have beyond dispute turned aside to things that cannot profit. All sin is against God; and to be sure every departure from any of these ways of his which he has enjoined us in the observance of it, is so. And there is a great deal of this to be found in the midst of us. And let me assure you, it is not a thing to be slighted or disregarded. As light a matter as we may make of it, and think what hurt is there in it, or what perils are we exposed to by it? Yet God reckons it a setting ourselves against him. Well, have we in this way done this through our folly? Yet have a care of continuing in this unhappy posture. Take heed of walking on in this contrariety, if nothing is done to remove it, God will charge it home on us; and what shall we expect at his hands if he so does this? Surely it will be *impar congressus*, the *damage will fall on us* and not on him. We must necessarily be the sufferers in the end, and not he. He will be too hard for us, there is all reason for us to consider on this before we begin. It is a question which he would have a sinful people study an answer to, Ezek. 22:14, "Can thine heart endure? Can thine hand be strong, in the day that I shall deal with thee?" Our impotency will never make a match for his omnipotence. What a call then is this to our speedy and undelayed returning to him? Are we set in opposition to the great God? Let us quit this station, and seek to be reconciled. It is the advice which is given in this regard, Isa. 7:5, "Let him take hold of my strength that he may make peace with me." And our only safety will be in following of it. Be we then advised to observe this counsel, and we shall find it for our good.

DOCTRINE 5:
God in punishing of such a people walks contrary to them.

In this way, he expresses the nature of the judgments which he brings on them for their willful impenitence, and by this manner of expression he vindicates the righteousness of his proceedings against them in the way of judgment. It is nothing else but a retaliation; he pays them in their own kind; and what can be more equal? For, if they set themselves against him, it is but just that he should be against them; if they are the aggressors, it is fit he vindicates himself, by withstanding them. It is true, if, when God brings a people into trouble, in their provoking him by their sinning against him, he sanctifies these troubles to them, they will have an abundant reason to confess it to his praise. David, therefore, confesses both the goodness of the affliction, and the faithfulness of God in inflicting it on him, Psa. 119:71, "It is good for me that I have been afflicted," and verse 75, "Thou in faithfulness hast afflicted me." And God many times has such a gracious design as this in work, Isa. 27:9, "By this shall the iniquity of Jacob be purged," and this is the point of this new fruit, to take away his sin. But as it not always proves so, to all that are visibly in the covenant; many are made worse instead of being bettered by their afflictions. So, it is uncertain what shall be the event, until the providence of God determines it, and it is equally certain that the judgments themselves are more ways than one to be reputed contrary to them. *For:*

I. In this he accomplishes the covenant threatening. If we look on the covenant of God as it is plighted between him and the body of a people professing to be his, it is very evident, that there do not only belong to it gracious promises made to their faithful obedience to him, but also awful threatenings against all disobedience; and to these threatenings belong all the afflictions that are denounced in the word of God against the disobedience of a people that stand in this way related to him. There are some indeed who do call these the promises of the covenant; but it is very *wrongly termed in that way*, if not a plain and laughable attempt at defining it as such. For a promise always has a respect to something that is good; where these things are in their own nature evil, and so the scripture calls them evil, which is the proper matter of a threatening; as in Jer. 11:17, "The Lord of hosts that planted thee, has pronounced evil against thee." And although sometimes eventually they prove for good, and that according to God's purpose, and on this account, those that are compared to good figs, are said to be sent to Babylon for their good, (Jer. 24:5). Yet this is besides their nature. God's children, therefore, are accustomed to be afraid of those judgments, (Psa. 119:120). And God therefore speaks of them, that he may stir up this fear, to make them cautious against exposing themselves to them.

2. Here, by them, God is said to hurt men. So, he expresses it in Joshua 24:20, "Then will he turn and do you hurt, and consume you, after that he has done you good." They are many ways which are harmful to a people that are brought under their impressions. Besides the misery that men personally suffer by them, in which some are usually more deeply concerned than others, being made the peculiar monuments of the severity of such judgments, there is great evil which befalls the body of such a people. They are greatly hurt by famines, by pestilences, by sword, by captivity and bondage, their glory is disgraced by such disasters, their numbers are wasted, and they are made, of a great many, to be but a few; their comforts of life are taken away from them, and they are brought into miserable distress. They are filled

with sorrows and bitter mournings; and they are wasted, impoverished, and brought low by them, and made to come down and sit in the dust solitary; they are made a reproach to their enemies, a scoff and a scorn to all those that hate them. These point at them and say, *this is Zion the out-cast, etc.* And all this very sensibly hurts them; and that which a man is hurt by, must necessarily be contrary to him.

3. These are all of them the effects and discoveries of God's anger. And that is certainly against them. Anger is one of the separating affections, and it makes a distance between him that is angry, and those at whom he is so. It is true, there may be a love in the foundation of these afflictions, and many times there is so, for he has said, Rev. 3:19, "As many as I love, I rebuke and chasten." In this there is a consistency between love and anger. A father may be angry with his offending son, and spank him in anger, but love governs that wrath. If love is in it, then all this is for them in the secret counsel of God. But the anger is certain, the course of providence bears witness to that; where there is not a present discovery of the love which is at work in the management of it. And besides, this love is usually reserved but for a remnant, for whom God has thoughts of peace, and to put a good end to their afflictions; whereas others are exposed to his force of indignation. But when God brings these evils on men, he is said to *make a way* for his anger, (Psalm 78:50). And how do we find in scripture, the history of such dispensations introduced with that preface, *viz.*, that the anger of the Lord was kindled against Israel, and therefore he did so

and so. And this tells us that God in this walks contrary to them.

4. And it is directly contrary to men's desire and hopes, as sin is opposite to God's holiness, and it grieves him, so is sorrow to men's inclinations, and it vexes them. Here such expressions are used to set it forth by, 2 Chron. 15:5-6, "Great vexations were on all the inhabitants of the countries; for God did vex them with all adversity." There is in all men naturally a desire and craving after felicity; they would, if possible, enjoy a wellbeing, according to their resentments of it; and although the fall has made them ignorant of what is their best good, yet they apprehend a goodness in peace, health, prosperity, credit, liberty, *etc.* These are agreeable to them, and therefore, they are naturally in love with them; and the hope of enjoying them, is that which nourishes in them, these endeavors which they lay out for the compassing and securing of them to themselves. That which is contrary to this, that undermines their peace and health, and destroys their prosperity and liberty, *etc.*, is that which they hate, and it perplexes them. And so, when God by his providence in this way deals with them, he crosses their aims, and cravings, and expectations, and in it he walks contrary to them.

Use. 1. This may point us to what interpretation to put on these judgments of God, which we for a long time been laboring under. God, of his rich grace, grant that in the winding up of all this, we may find by an happy experience, that there has been love in them all. And that will only be when they prove to be the blessed means of our thorough reformation, when by them our iniquities shall be purged away from us. But let us know and be assured, that if we remain impenitent under them, there is but very little sign of this for the present. And this is certain, that as long as God is in this way with us, we have him for our adversary, and so the prophet interpreted in, Lam. 2:4, "He stood with his right hand as an adversary." He is setting of himself against us. He and we are facing one another; we by our impenitence are confronting him, and he by his judgments is withstanding us. We are provoking him to jealousy by our sins, and he is provoking us to jealousy by his strokes, so it is expressed in, Deut. 32:21. And if we do not put this sense on the present state of affairs, we shall deceive ourselves, and be exposed to more of his wrath; and is not this a fearful thing?

Use 2. Let it put us on serious and solemn thoughts of making our peace with him. Has God been so showing himself to us that he is in good earnest? Has he begun to put his threatenings in execution on us? And have we felt no little part of their pain, in the many frowns of providence that we have labored under? It is high time then for us to think to ourselves, and be in good earnest too, and trifle no longer with him. It was indeed high presumption in us to dare him to this at first; and to stout it out so long against his warnings with which he sought to reclaim us that a further proceeding against us might so have been prevented. But it will be madness to a sudden recurrence for us to continue in it, when we see him up in arms, and causing the arrows of his vengeance to fly among us, and he is marching through our land in his fury. It is high time then for us to enter into a serious consultation whether there is no way to be found in which an end may be put to such a controversy, and without delay to get into the way. For, if he sets himself against us, *woe unto us*, we can never stand before him. Is he angry? Remember who has said, Psalm 76:7, "Thou, even thou art to be feared, and who may stand in thy sight when once thou art angry?" This then is our present business, the work that the day calls us to, and let us be awakened diligently to attend on it. It is better for Christians to fall down at his feet by a true repentance, than to fall before him by his terrible judgments. None ever resisted him and prospered. If his hand takes hold on vengeance, he will surely recompence vengeance to his adversaries.

DOCTRINE 6:
There is a certain gradation in the judgments of God on an apostatizing people.

God here speaks of punishing them, or smiting them (for so the word used in our text firstly signifies) seven times more, *i.e.* by a seven-fold greater and more terrible pain than that which was before, and he mentions this many times over in the context, in every one of which he still rises by sevens. Seven is not here to be taken strictly, but for *many*, or much greater; and yet, it being a number of perfection, it denotes a very notable and observable augmentation of the calamities threatened, in the progress of God's judicial dispensations, when he passes over from one scene of judgments to another, and with it points us to the gradual progress which he is pleased to make with men this way, and this gives us the advantage to take notice of the accustomed dealings of God with a people in covenant with him. This is different from what is usually towards those that are strangers to him, or towards particular persons. And there are four things that we may here take notice of, only remembering, that God uses much of his sovereignty in the diversifying of his dispensations on this account, as to circumstances, though for the substance this is the ordinary course.

1). He is accustomed first to give them warning before he strikes them. These judgments come for sin, and that according to the threatening. But God being merciful, and pitiful, does not fall on them presently on their every prevarication; but, though they give him provocation, he will first offer them admonition. He tells them what they have done, how they have exposed themselves by it. He tells them he is loath to strike them if they will be reclaimed on easier terms, and accordingly invites them to it. And these warnings are first gentler, and afterwards more severe; and that is when he not only cautions, but with it threatens them in case they will not presently comply with them. And the reason of all this is, because, if they will by any fair means, or hard words be reclaimed, there may be a stop to it, and the threatenings not take place on them. The reason why he proceeds to strike them, is rendered to be because they did not take these warnings; what does God himself say in Zeph. 3:7, "I said, surely thou wilt fear me, thou wilt receive instruction." And see how God interprets his own threatenings, Jer. 18:7-8, "At what time I speak concerning a nation, to pluck up, and pull down and destroy; if that nation turn from their evil, I will repent of the evil that I thought to do to them." Repentance is here ascribed to him *after the manner of men*; the meaning is, *I will not do it.* He limits the threatening to this hypothesis. God has that respect for his people, that if chiding will do, he will not strike them. If words will prevail, he will not proceed to blows. It is therefore said that he does not afflict willingly, and this work of punishing them is called his *strange work*. Whereas he many times comes on others suddenly, and they are surprised and cut off without any fore-warning given them.

2). When he does strike, he does not do it all at once. He does not cut off his people at one stroke, though they have given him provocation enough to do it. He does not begin and make an end at the same time, and by the same judgment by which he first afflicted them. But if ever it must come to that, by reason of their woeful obstinacy and refusing to receive correction by his afflictive providences, there is a very considerable time in which that is doing; and many leisurely steps are taken before it arrives at this. When God threatens Nineveh, we find how it is expressed, Nahum 1:9, he will "make an utter end. Affliction shall not rise up the second time." Where it is observable in our text, laid by the context, that there is a process from one to another, and from that to another, and there is a long time which passes before the evil is finished, and the last scene brought in. And if we observe, we shall find, that it was so long, after God had begun in his judgments with his backsliding people of old, before they came to be pulled up and destroyed, that the prophets begun to be mocked, and the people grew into such security, that they concluded it should never be, and begun to make bold challenges about it. Now the reason of God's using this method is because he is in a way of discipline with his people. He is trying if they will be amended by his rods, and therefore, in wisdom, he proves another course, when one fails of doing the work, so that, if there may be any hope, they may not perish at last, but be led to repentance. It says that he is very loath to destroy them if it may be prevented by such courses as are proper.

3). He is also accustomed to begin with lesser, and more tolerable strokes. He does not come to the extremity at once, he proves them first with rods, before he proceeds to make use of scorpions in punishing of them. And there is a double consideration under which this may be observed; it is either with respect to the judgments themselves, or to the degrees in which he doth inflict them. Here we have such a difference mentioned, Isa. 9:1, "When at first he lightly afflicted," *etc.,* and afterwards "did more grievously" afflict her. There are some afflictions which in themselves are far less formidable than others; the nature of man is not so affrighted at them, and on this there is not so great a discovery of the anger of God, at least as to its heat. We find David chose rather to fall into the hands of God than of men, and God many times begins with such; these are the forlorn of his army which are first sent up to alarm a sinning people. He brings on them the scarcity of the comforts of this life, by cutting short the fruits of the earth, and he visits them with epidemic sicknesses, by which they are brought low, and the like. There are also several degrees in the same kinds of afflictions, by which they prove, more or less, distressing to a people. And God uses this to begin at the lower degrees, where he comes first as a moth to the house of Ephraim, (Hosea 5:12). He diminishes them, and shortens their comforts, brings difficulties and straits on them, before he falls on them in its severity. He brings scarcity before a killing famine, gentler sicknesses before destroying pestilences, *etc.* And the reason of this is, because he will prove them to see if their hearts are tender, and sensible of the easier touches of his anger, that if they so be, there may be an end, and no further process made in the way of his wrath against them.

4). But if the easier corrections will not do, he then goes on to strike them harder. If his hand may be stopped from this, it is good. But, if it is not, he is not accustomed to tarry always where he was, and do no more, but he will, in due season, go a step further, and make them to undergo greater and more grievous calamities, he doubles his strokes, and pulls up the floodgates higher, and makes the gap in the hedge wider, so that their plagues become great and astonishing. And this is observable in a terrible respect; he does it, partly by greatening the same strokes, and so adding to its degrees, partly by bringing in of greater and more terrible judgments, such as are more frightful to men, and which carry in them more of his indignation, and in their own nature are dreadful. If scarcity and sickness will not do, if famines, and pestilences do not prevail, he calls for a wasting sword on his land, and gives it a commission to devour, and make itself drunk with the blood of the slain. Partly also by heaping up of manifold calamities at once on them, involving of them in all sorts of difficulties, as, Ezek. 14:21, "How much more when I send my four sore judgments on Jerusalem, the sword, and the famine, and the noisome beasts, and the pestilence." And these lay all waste before them, and they that escape the one, are devoured of the other, and now they are terribly distressed. Here, how are all terrible miseries heaped together in the last step of this progress in our context? (verse 29, *etc.*). And so it is expressed in Deut. 28:61, "Also every sickness, and every plague," *etc.,* "them will the Lord bring on thee, until thou be destroyed."

Use. 1. We may from this take a rule to judge our present state by. This manner of God's dealing has been observably exemplified on us; such a progress as this we have been under. And it is now a long time since God has begun it, and it continues unto this day. How gradually has our God been going with us? How many steps has he taken? And how are our calamities grown and increased? And to this day they remain on us, and still look if they were on the growing hand. It is a great many years since God begun to signalize his displeasure against this people, and, as he has been exceedingly patient with us, in that he is to this day gotten no further, notwithstanding all that we have done to provoke him to it; so he has been progressive with us; how often has he changed his providences? And to what a height are our perplexities grown? Nor is there yet a cessation. May we not say as it is in, Isa. 9:12, "For all this his anger is not turned away, but his hand is stretched out still." And what is the matter of instruction that we have to learn from it? May it not well be that which follows, verse 13, "For the people returneth not to him that smiteth them." God surely has been following the hypothesis laid down in our text. It is because we are still walking contrary to him and will not come to an amendment with him. Let it then leave conviction on us and tell us that we are not as we should be, otherwise God would have been otherwise to us than he is. And this should awaken us to consider what we have to do.

Use. 2. Let us then see and admire at the wonderful patience of God expressed to us in it. Surely, though we have cause deeply to be abased to think that it should be so with us as it is; yet we have deserved other, and a worse manner of dealing from him. And though there is severity to be taken notice of in this, yet there is a great deal of lenity intermixed with it. If he had cut us off as soon as we begun to revolt from him, and given us no advantage at all to have made our peace with him, it had been just, and we could never have laid any injurious dealing to his charge. That he makes so many steps in it, and that he proceeds, so slowly in them all, is to be cordially and thankfully acknowledged by us; and we have reason to say, "it is of the Lord's mercy that we are not consumed," (Lam. 3:22). As then there is a great awakening in it to put us on diligent seeking to him, so there is abundant encouragement for us so to do. We may rationally argue from this, that he who afflicts us so unwillingly, would very willingly have his hands held by us, and, as it were wonders that we are so foolish that we take no more care to do it. Consider *then:*

Use. 3. Let it rouse us all up to this reformation. You here see how it is; we have a holy God with which to do, who is jealous for his great name. And though he has a reserve of mercy for the penitent, yet he will have his honor in all his works. He has been apparently testifying his displeasure against our ways and doings, and he is still growing on us in it, and we cannot see to the other end of these dark dispensations. Why then should we be so stiff-necked and hard hearted? What good shall we get by a resolute pursuance of our own ways, against all the endeavors that are laid out on us to reduce us from them? Have we not felt enough already to our sorrow? And shall we force him to lay more and heavier calamities on us still? O! let us be wise! It was good advice that Pharaoh's servants gave to him, Exod. 10:7, "How long shall this man be a snare to us? Let the men go," *etc.,* "knowest thou not yet that Egypt is destroyed?" And may I not well say, how long shall our sins fool us? How long shall we stand by them, and not part with them? Do we not know that they have already almost ruined us? Remember then, that though God has gone far with us in his judgments, and increased them more than once on us, yet there are more and more terrible ones behind, ready to be poured out on us? He has not shot all his arrows yet; the sharpest are still in his quiver; and he seems to have a fearful one now on the string. And shall we not fall down at his feet and prevent it? Shall we yet dare him to it, and force him to make us feel the bitterest of it? O! let it not once be!

DOCTRINE 7:
God is accustomed to use intermissions in his afflicting of a people that will not reform under his judgments.

When he begins in a way of judgment with them; when he takes his rod in hand and strikes them, and they are not bettered by these blows, yet as he proceeds very slowly in renewing and adding severity to his strokes, according as was observed under the former doctrine, so he makes many stops and delays in his progress, although he takes them out of one fire and kindles another on them, as he threatens to do by them, (Ezek. 15:7). Yet, he has his intervals between them. The manner of expression in the text notes that God seeks, and consequently waits for their reformation by these things, and that signifies such an intermission as this. And there are two things in which it will be more especially seen.

1. He does not speedily pass from one judgment to another. When he brings one sort of affliction on his people, as a testimony of his displeasure at them, he continues them under that for a considerable time, before he goes on to another. We read of a famine in David's time that continued for three years successively; and no other judgment is recorded to intervene, though its procuring cause was not presently removed, (2 Sam. 21). And so in Elisha's time of a famine which lasted three years, by which Israel, under Ahab's wicked reign

was distressed, (1 Kings 18:1). And of one that lasted seven years in the days of Elisha, in the time when Joram, Ahab's son, reigned, (2 Kings 8:1). And the reason why God does this is because he will wait to see what efficacy this will have before he takes a further course with them. He does not come to kill them, but to cure them, if it may be. And here he acts like a wise physician, who, when he has administered a proper sort of medicine, will wait for its working, a competent time, not looking that it will work, as soon as it is down. And if one medicine will not do, he will give another of the same, and it may be a larger dose of it. Before he leaves that off, he will go about to try any other experiment. He does not presently say this will not do, though it does not immediately appear in its desirable effects. God says, it may be that they will think about all this themselves, and lay this judgment to heart. And by its continuance they may be brought to solemn consideration, which may set them on reformation. Therefore, until the judgment comes to be notoriously despised by them, he many times continues them under its exercise.

    2. And he sometimes gives them a present deliverance, and respite from the troubles which they have been exercised with. There are very frequently lucid intervals to be observed in the course of God's providence towards a sinning people, whom he has under the rod, and this notwithstanding they do not answer the end of these afflictions, but abide in their degeneracy. He does not always grieve them, but, though they do not hearken to him; though they do not cease to provoke him, but are senseless, careless, and go

on in their way, yet he extends a great deal of his pity to them, he remembers their frame, and he interposes some great deliverance or other, and by this tries them between with his mercy; to see if in this way he may break their hearts with kindness, and let them experience how unwilling he is to do them hurt, if they do not force him to it. Here he causes the stormy clouds which hand over them, and showered trouble on them to break, and some beams of light and comfort to dart in between; and all to try if mercy after judgment will do anything with them; if his being beforehand in his kindness to them, will melt their hard hearts into a compliance with his calls and counsels. And by this at least he will leave them the more inexcusable if they yet persist in their obstinacy. In this way we find that in Ahab's reign, though the foregoing famine had not worked the expected reformation, and God brought a sword after it; yet God gave Israel two signal victories over the Syrians, who had sorely distressed them, (1 Kings 20). And then in Joram's reign, God succored that people with a strange relief in a grievous famine and frightened away their enemies, when they were just ready to swallow them up, (2 Kings 7). And again, afterwards in the days of Jeroboam the second, of which we have that observable passage, 2 Kings 14:24-26, "He did that which was evil," *etc.* "He restored the coast of Israel," *etc.* "For the Lord saw the affliction of Israel," *etc.* And many times God has done things after this manner with his people, when the entertainment they have given to his judgments has been a provocation to him to do otherwise.

Use 1. Learn from this how unreasonable a thing it is for such a people to maintain their rebellion against God. What reason can there possibly be given for their refusing to return to him, and reform the things that give him offense? How wonderfully God in this shows his tenderness and great compassion towards them? And one would think it should be enough to melt hearts of *adamant.* That the hardest flint should dissolve under its influence. What greater provocation can there be given to God, than to have his word despised, and rod condemned, and a people under the experiment of both, obstinately stopping their ears and hardening their hearts? This is enough to put him on resolving to spare them no more, to turn his rod into a sword, and pass from correction to vengeance, and cut them off at once. And shall he, for all this, hold back his hand when it is up, and show his great kindness to a people that are not affected with his judgment? Shall he endeavor in this way to win them, after he has afflicted them to no purpose? And shall they for all, and after this persist in their former evil courses? May he not call on heaven and earth to be astonished at this? How horrible and amazing a thing must it needs be?

Use. 2. Let it put us on the trial in this regard. Has not our God dealt in this way by us more than once or twice? Have there not been very notable respites which he has afforded to us in the midst of our troubles? Has he not mercifully given us several breathing times, and these considerable, between one calamity and another? And what improvement is it that we have made of them? Did we not begin to hope that he was in the way of returning again to us? But have there not new clouds risen again afterwards, and showered down a fresh tempest on us? May we not use the words which the prophet does in the name of his people? Jer. 8:15, "We looked for peace, but behold no good; and for a time of health, and behold trouble." And it is good for us to enquire when this is. Surely if we had rightly understood the things of our peace, and accordingly improved such an opportunity wisely, it would not have been so. If, when God looked as if he were coming towards us in a way of mercy, we had cordially returned to him in a way of repentance and reformation, those acts of deliverance, would have been the day break of our salvations, and God would have established us in his favor. Let the thought then of this, convince us of our grievous folly, and lay us low before God. Alas! Did we not begin arrogantly to say, the bitterness of death is over? To think that now the judgments of God were at an end, and we should see no more of them? And on this to grow the more confident, and secure, and remorseless, and so to forget the obligations lying on us, and on this to promise ourselves to enjoy peace, though we continued in our old way and course? Yes, and here have we thrown by our thoughts of reformation, supposing that all matters stood right and well between God and us? Is it not so? And if so it is, how righteously has God dealt with us, in raising up of new troubles, and bringing us into more perplexing calamities than before? How must our mouths be stopped, and the holiness of God be adored by us in this respect? Certainly, the face of providence calls aloud, for our putting of ourselves on such a trial; and let us account it our interest to comply with it solemnly.

DOCTRINE 8:
As long as a professing people remain unreformed, God will proceed in his judgments against them.

This is the very sum and substance of the threatening contained in our text. And it is three times besides repeated in our context. There may be many changes in the process which God is using with such a people, and he may see meet now and then to give them some intermissions in that process. And in this he acts in his own sovereign pleasure. But for all this he will not so put an end to their troubles, nor is it to be expected. There are two things contained in this doctrine. *Consider:*

1. That there will be a proceeding in the way of judgments. When God begins to take such a course with them, he will hold on in it, as long as they hold on in a course of impenitence and obstinacy. And though he has kept them never so long under them, yet if there is no repentance, no reformation employed on them by all, he will not so leave off, but will add still more to afflict them. He will proceed in his way, as long as they proceed in theirs. We find, that when God had enumerated how many several courses he had taken with Israel to reclaim them, and all had proved unsuccessful, and that is the remark which is made at the foot of every one of them, "yet have ye not returned unto me saith the Lord," Amos 4:6. *etc.* He gives them leave to understand that he will

go on, and therefore bids them to look and prepare for it, verse 12, "Therefore thus will I do unto thee O Israel; and because I will do this unto thee, prepare to meet thy God, O Israel." He is saying, look for it, make ready; it shall certainly be.

2. That there will be an increasing or aggravating of these troubles. There shall not only be a continuance, but an augmentation; they shall meet with more and more severe; they shall be plagued yet deeper and deeper, and inextricably into their afflictions and distresses. He threatens to lay aside all pity, Jer. 13:14, "I will not have pity, nor mercy, but destroy them." Ezek. 5:11, "Neither shall mine eye spare, nor will I have any pity." And this is intended, in his punishing of them seven times. And the ground of his thus proceeding will appear, in the consideration of these things.

1). A professing covenant people are under greatest obligations to glorify God, which is done by their faithful obedience to his commands. It is for this that God has formed them into a people, under such circumstances, Isa. 43:21, "this people have I formed for myself, they shall show forth my praise." God requires it of them, and expects it from them; he does not look for it from others to whom he has not so revealed himself, but he says of such a people for whom he has done so much, more than for others, *surely they will serve me, and honor me.*

2). When such a people degenerate, they fall from the great end which they were enjoined, and every way advantaged to serve to, and so they dishonor instead of honoring him. And the truth is, there are none in the world that reflect so much of dishonor on God, as such Christians do. All the sin and wickedness of a heathen people does not bring so much reproach to his name, as the backslidings of such in his church. His name suffers more by them, than by all the profligate abominations of those who are strangers to the covenant, because his name is not so much concerned in them. And therefore, when these do the very same things for the matter of them, which the heathen do, they do a great deal worse than these, and the reason of it is because it is *they* that do it.

3). Learn by their apostasy they render themselves unprofitable. And there are none more so than they. All the cost, and care, and peculiar husbandry that God has laid out on them is lost; he has been at a great deal more of expense on his vineyard, than on the vast wilderness; he has fenced it, cleared it, and planted it, and afforded it a great deal of special tendency and this, as to any fruit which they bring forth for him, is thrown away on it. God on this account compares his people to a vine, which is a sort of plant, that if it bear well, and good grapes plentifully, is very excellent and useful. But if it does not so bear, it is good for nothing but to make a fire of, (Ezek. 15:1ff). Other trees, though they do not bear fruit, yet they may serve for many other uses, but the vine is altogether unserviceable in any other way but this.

4). God in afflicting of them, uses means, if it may be obtained, that he may bring them to their fruitfulness again. While they enjoyed times of peace and prosperity, and all things went according to their desire, they grew corrupt and left off to bring forth fruit to his praise. Now, these afflictive providences which he brings on them, were his pruning and cutting of them. He by this pares off their excrescencies, and lets them bleed, and this, if anything, looks as if it were probable to recover them again. That this is the direct design of these judgments, in this appears, because God says, if *they are not reformed by these things*, and that plainly intimates, that reformation was the thing that was looked for by them. And for this reason we shall find him so often complaining of them, because this was not the effect following on them, see Isa. 1:5, "Why should ye be smitten any more? Ye will revolt more and more," and, Jer. 2:30, "In vain have I smitten your children; they would not receive correction." Now a thing is then said to be in vain, when the end of it is frustrated.

5). Consider, as long as they do not remain bettered by this, their benefit and his glory is concerned in his proceeding further in the course of his judgments. Their benefit is deeply interested in it. For they are no more bettered by these afflictions, until they are carried up to reformation. The medicine that is administered to men, does not work for them, as long as it irritates the disease, and makes the sickness and evil disposition to work more strongly, but does not remove them. Then it works kindly, when it conquers the malady. And truly, if God leaves off afflicting before such a people are reformed, they are apt to be by it more hardened; and when God is weary of striking them by reason of their obstinacy, it is a sad sign that he is about to give them up as desperate, (Isa. 1:5; Psa. 81:11-12 and 95:10-11). And when God lays by his rod after he has been using it, before his people are amended, it bodes that he intends next to take up the sword, when he has let them alone a while without check to fill up their measure. His glory also is here concerned; he is honor bound to bear a testimony against the apostasies of his people; and he must and will be at length too hard for them, one way or other his glory is trampled on by their impenitence, his holiness cannot endure that it is always so. And therefore, we are told that if after all endeavors, and utmost patience drawn forth into long suffering, their returning is not obtained, at last it must come to extirpation, and scattering of them into the corners of the earth. The sum is, either God's name must suffer, or else a people that are departed from their covenant obligations, and will by no means be reformed, must be cut off. And so they are made the monuments of his righteous revenge, because they would not, hearken to his voice, Matthew 23:37-38, "How often would I have gathered you, but you would not; behold your house is left unto you desolate."

    Use 1. This truth gives us a sad prognostic of a people that are left to insensibleness and hardness of heart, under the blows of God. It tells us how miserable they are likely to be. We are here given to understand that if they are resolved, God is resolved too. If they say there is no hope, but we will follow our own ways, and will not forsake them, God will also say, there is no hope, but you must see and feel the weight of the hand of his displeasure, and be made the monuments of his stupendous wrath. The best that is to be concluded concerning such a people, is that they are likely to be made to feel more amazing judgments, than before, there is no hope of an end being put to them, unless it comes to that, that he is done striving with them in this way; and that is abundantly more formidable. And although God can, if he will, break their hearts after all, and when no means will do it, yet his Spirit is able to melt them down, and cast them anew. And sometimes he exalts his sovereign grace in doing it, as, Isa. 57:18, "I smote him, and he went on frowardly; I have seen his ways and will heal him." Yet this is arbitrary with him; if they belong to his election of grace, it shall be so; but that is a secret thing; but as to the present posture of things, and referring to the articles of the covenant between God and such a people, it speaks sadly, and woefully bodes that their calamities are but begun on them. We may count from the breaking out of his displeasure, but who shall live to see the quenching of it, God alone knows; and whether it may at last end graciously or not, we may expect to see God acting in fearful tragedies among them before he has completed everything, and we may be sure that he will either hew them, or break them in pieces.

Use 2. Let it then solemnly call on us, seriously to think of, and speedily to improve this truth to a thorough reformation. Let us take it to be a voice from heaven to awaken us this day to the practice of this duty. God has now for a long time been calling us aloud to reformation; and that by many ways and courses that he has been practicing with us. How many years since he put it into the mouths of his servants to complain of the degenerating of this people, from the spirit and design of those that were first employed in the planting of these churches? How many years is it since there have been convincing and openly confessed witnesses in the providence of God, to the displeasure he had taken at that degeneracy? And does he not continue these tokens to this day? But our ears have been sealed; and though we have been under some consternations, especially when some distressing affliction has broken in on us, yet how little is there done meanwhile, towards the putting an end to God's controversy? God is still onward in his way, and proceeding from one step to another, and going forward to punish us more and more, and shall we never be instructed? O! when shall it once be? Is there nothing to be done at such a day as this is? Are all things right? Have there been no open and notorious declensions from God among us? Or are we recovered out of them? Is everything among us as it should be? *Why then is his hand stretched out still?* What is the meaning of the continuing and blowing up of the heat of his anger? And is it nobody's work to begin in this matter? Or is it not everyone's business to set about it in his place? If we are in a private capacity, and cannot actively influence the public so as to mend it, yet may we not mend *one thing?* Are there not our personal iniquities in the heap or ephah? Or have we carried it so evenly and holily as to be altogether clear of this guilt? Who of us is there that dares to appear, and own that we have done nothing to the continuance of these judgments? And if everyone would do that which is to be done at home in this regard, it would surely contribute not a little to a general reformation. And we may by a holy exemplary conversation, and earnest prayers to God, help forward this work. If we are in a public station, and there advantaged peculiarly to put forward such a work, shall we look one on another, and strain complements, who shall begin in it? Shall we not further join hearts, and hands, and counsels in this business? Shall any of us draw back, and refuse to be concerned in it; or shall we withstand it? Note that man an enemy to God and his people. I shall not here enlarge in enumerating the catalogue of those things that desire to be looked into and after in this reformation, but earnestly wish that it may be a matter of solemn consultation and enquiry. Only let me say, this work must be done sooner or later: God expects it, he calls aloud for it, he says that he will have it. And what will it advantage us to dally and delay, until God has multiplied his judgments on us, and made us a by word and an astonishment to the world? We should assure ourselves it may be worse, but it will not be really better with us, until we come roundly to this work. Why then should we provoke a good and a gracious God to more wrath, and pull down on our own heads more of his fearful judgments? Stop him now; otherwise ruin may be not far off. We have tried our carnal policy already, and have found it nothing to avail us, but rather to entangle us in greater perplexities, and more inextricable. Let us now essay the spiritual policy. Resolve we, from this day forward to make diligent search after, and utterly to renounce all our sins; to return as one man to the Lord; and set ourselves in good earnest about this work. And I dare say, God will be jealous for the land, and pity his people; and then will he arise as a strong man after new wine, plead our cause for us, and bring us forth out of darkness into the light, set our feet on a rock, and put a new song into our mouths, even praise unto our God. Amen.

FINIS

Other Helpful Books on Reformation by Puritan Publications

God's Covenant and Our Duty
by Samuel Willard (1640-1707)

The Covenant of Redemption
by Samuel Willard (1640-1707)

Vain Imaginations in the Worship of God
by Samuel Willard, Jonathan Dickinson, Joshua Moodey, Nathan Stone and Jonathan Edwards

5 Marks of Biblical Reformation
by C. Matthew McMahon

The Duty of Reformation in Light of God's Mercies
by Thomas Gouge (1605-1681)

Reformation and Desolation
by Stephen Marshall (1594–1655)

The Christian's Duty Towards Reformation
by Thomas Ford (1598–1674)

The Precious Seeds of Reformation
by Humphrey Hardwicke (n.d.)

A Discourse on Church Discipline and Reformation
by Daniel Cawdrey (1588-1664)

Family Reformation Promoted, and Other Works
by Daniel Cawdrey (1588-1664)

Church Reformation Tenderly Handled
by John Brinsley (1600-1665)

Gradual Reformation Intolerable
by C. Matthew McMahon and Anthony Burgess (1600-1663)

www.ingramcontent.com/pod-product-compliance
Lightning Source LLC
Chambersburg PA
CBHW070205100426
42743CB00013B/3060